GEOFFREY WILLS

Collecting Copper and Brass

Drawings by A. J. TURVEY

BELL PUBLISHING COMPANY • NEW YORK

Acknowledgements

Thanks are due to the following for kindly allowing the reproduction of photographs: the Earl of Mount Edgcumbe for plates 4, 8, 14, 16, 20, 21 and 22; Dr. F. A. Turk for plate 13; the Victoria and Albert Museum, London, for plates 3, 5, 6, 9, 17 and 18; Brighton Corporation for plate 10; Plymouth Museum and Art Gallery for plate 19; and the Royal Institution of Cornwall, Truro, for plates 7 and 23.

© Geoffrey Wills MCMLXII
This edition published by Bell Publishing Company, Inc.,
a division of Crown Publishers, Inc.,
by arrangement with MacGibbon & Kee, Ltd.

a b c d e f g h

Printed in the United States of America

Contents

Foreword

Part One: Copper and its alloys

1 Mining and manufacture	13
2 Alloys—composition and uses	21
3 Countries in which copper alloys have been used	28

Part Two: A dictionary of articles made from copper and its alloys — 59

Appendix A: Fakes	146
Appendix B: Cleaning	149
Index	151

Foreword

ARTICLES have been made from copper and its alloys for many thousands of years, and there seems every probability that they will continue to be so made for thousands more. In this book an attempt is made to describe as many of them as possible, to give the reader an idea of how copper is obtained and treated for manufacture, and to outline the history of the use of the metal in numerous countries.

Some of the quotations from old books and newspapers have been modernized in spelling and punctuation to make it easier to follow what are, without doubt, the most interesting and helpful descriptions of eighteenth century and earlier events and processes.

PART ONE

Copper and its alloys

CHAPTER ONE

Mining and manufacture

COPPER is an element, in the words of the Oxford Dictionary: 'One of the simple substances of which all material bodies are compounded'. It was known to the ancient alchemists by the sign of the planet Venus, ♀, and its name comes from the Roman *Cyprium aes*: 'bronze from Cyprus,' an island once noted for supplies of the metal. It is found occasionally pure, when it is known as Native or Virgin Copper, and in the form of a number of minerals, and it was almost certainly the first metal known to Man.

Copper is obtainable not only by mining, but it can be precipitated in the presence of iron. There are a number of springs suitable for this in different parts of the world, and two of them in Hungary are referred to by an author writing about 150 years ago. He said that these particular waters are 'so richly impregnated with copper and sulphuric acid, that iron thrown into them is dissolved by the acid, and the copper falls to the bottom in its metallic form. Near these springs, pits are dug, and filled with the water: old iron is then thrown into them, which, in about a fortnight or three weeks, is taken out, and copper scraped off. By this process, a hundred pounds of iron will produce from eighty to ninety pounds of copper.' Credulous people thought at that time that the iron was actually transmuted into copper. Pure copper will form also under other conditions, and mines that have been abandoned and re-opened after an interval are found sometimes with their woodwork encrusted heavily with crystals of the glittering reddish metal.

The actual mining of copper ores was a much more troublesome business than throwing a piece of iron into water, and changed very little from the most primitive times until comparatively modern days. The processes of mining and smelting were described, and illustrated clearly with excellent woodcuts, by Agricola (a German named Georg Bauer, who wrote under the Latinized form of his surname) in a book published in 1556 called *De re metallica*. In it, he recorded all that was known at the time on the subject, and it is clear that not only was the actual mining a laborious process but the extracting of the metal from the ore was a series of slow and lengthy operations. It was costly in materials, and in human effort and life.

In England, by the seventeenth century the ores near the surface had become exhausted, and tunnelling below became necessary. Progress downwards was limited only by the efficiency of the apparatus for removing water that flooded in increasingly as the depth grew greater. As an eighteenth-century writer noted with truth: 'Copper being placed in the more interior strata of the earth, requires great skill in hydraulicks and mechanicks.' Early pumps for this essential work were horse- or man-operated and very primitive in construction and action; not only were they poor in performance, but they took heavy toll of those working at them.

A typical machine was the so-called Rag and Chain Pump. This was no more than a heavy iron chain with lumps of rag and leather fixed to it at intervals, and these were pulled through a tube measuring anything up to twenty-two feet in length. The end of the tube stood in the water, and as the rag and leather 'pistons' came up the tube, raised by means of the brute force of the men pulling at the chain, which was endless and ran round wheels at top and bottom, the water was brought up. A contemporary description of this crude device concluded as follows: 'The men work at it naked excepting their loose trowsers, and suffer much in their health and strength from the violence of the labour.' The same writer noted that a four-inch diameter Rag and Chain Pump needed five or six men every six hours to draw water to a height of twenty feet, and that their pay could be reckoned at £2 or £2 10s per month.

Steam power was available from the early years of the eighteenth century, when Thomas Savery's engine, recommended by the inventor himself in a pamphlet entitled *The Miner's Friend*, was built and used. It was an extremely uneconomical machine as it not only used great quantities of coal, but its water-raising power was limited severely by the pressure of steam generated. This, in turn, depended on the amount of heat applied to the boiler; which, if too great would melt the solder used in constructing this essential part of the apparatus. Savery's engine was superseded in due course by the introduction of that of Thomas Newcomen, which was an improvement in many respects but still required large quantities of fuel. For the Cornish copper mines, far from any coal fields, this was a great drawback, and even the fact that the government in 1741 allowed them their coal free of duty for working 'Fire Engines' did not result in an immediate increase in their use.

It was not until James Watt invented his version of the steam engine, a big improvement on those of any of his predecessors, that a noticeable extension of mechanical power took place in the copper mines. Not only did this engine give increased power and greater reliability, but it did so on a markedly reduced consumption of coal. So much so, indeed, that Watt installed the engines on hire, with the rental based on a percentage of the saving of fuel compared with what one of the old engines would have consumed to do the same amount of work.

After the ore had been brought to the surface it was sorted and crushed, and then awaited purchase by the smelters. Apart from occasional unsuccessful enterprises in other parts of England this was a distinct section of the metal trade, and was centred on South Wales from about 1720. There, principally in the Swansea district, with ample supplies of coal near at hand, and the Midlands metal-goods manufacturers equally accessible, it stayed and prospered for a century and a half. Earlier, the ore had been smelted on a small scale with charcoal as fuel, but an increasing scarcity of timber led to experiments in the use of coal. The actual smelting of the ore consisted of a series of roastings and re-roastings to drive-off and separate impurities; which included sulphur, arsenic, antimony and iron. The resulting product was a block or plate of pure copper, or of copper as pure in content as the knowledge of the time could make it.

The principal metals with which copper was alloyed are Tin and Zinc. The former was mined in a manner similar to copper, in the case of Cornwall and elsewhere was found in the same area, and the ore was treated afterwards in much the same way. Zinc, however, the basis of brass, was obtained in the form of a mineral known as Lapis Calaminaris, or Calamine. This ore of zinc was described by a writer as 'a mineral substance of a greyish, brownish, yellowish, or pale reddish colour, and sometimes of all these colours variously mixed'; which may not lead to identification easily by the reader.

Calamine has been found in many parts of the world, in Somerset and Nottinghamshire in seventeenth-century England, but the principal European sources were the Liége district of Belgium, and Germany. For use, the ore was roasted so that it could be reduced more easily to a powder, in which state it was mixed with the copper. The actual making of brass was described as follows in 1670: 'In one oven they set eight pots or pipkins at once, and let them be warm and hot, and when they are so, they take them out quickly and put the calaminaris in them, also they have a shovel made on purpose, that therewith they may take up and know how to distribute near 46 pounds in such eight pots. Then they lay in every pot upon the Lapis Calaminaris eight pounds of small broken copper pieces, and set in the pots again, and they let them stand nine hours in great heat, and in this nine hours are to be taken one heap and a half of coals, and when such coals are burnt out, then stir the stuff in the pot with an iron.' The molten alloy was poured between two large flat stones, left to cool, and in due course a plate of brass was the product. Alternatively, it was moulded into blocks.

In spite of the fact that Far Eastern metalworkers had known for centuries how to obtain pure zinc from Calamine, knowledge of the process was not discovered in England until 1738. It was thereafter possible to alloy it directly with copper for making brass, but perhaps on account of the higher cost of this method the process noted above remained in use until the Victorian age.

Until the end of the seventeenth century, if a flat sheet of metal was needed it was sometimes cast, which was not always satisfactory, or more often it was hammered. The hammering was accomplished either by a series of tools operated by water-power, or by a single hand-wielded hammer. The process was known at the time as battering, hence the Mineral and Battery Works formed in 1568, and the finished sheet was known sometimes as Battery metal. Hammering or battering was superseded by rolling blocks of metal between heavy cylinders repeatedly until it was of the required thickness, but the original process continued in use for the shaping of pans, kettles, and other articles for which it was appropriate.

The most widespread alternative to beating metal into shape was to cast it from a mould into which it was poured while molten. This process was especially suitable for bronze and brass, but copper exudes gases when it is hot, causing a pitted surface and a strong tendency to enclose small bubbles in the interior. For this reason, copper was seldom cast, but articles were made from its alloys by this process from very early times, and stone moulds dating back to the Bronze Age have been found.

For making works of art, primarily in bronze, the most important method is that of casting by *cire perdue*: literally, 'lost wax'. In this, the artist modelled his original in wax on a core of clay which had been shaped first roughly to the outline of the finished piece. The completed model was then enclosed in a casing of clay in which holes were left for the entry of molten metal, and for the escape of the wax when heated. This latter took place first, the metal was poured in, and when cooled the casting was removed and the core of clay inside it chipped away. Finally, the surface of the article was finished smoothly by chiselling and filing to remove imperfections and traces of the holes by which the metal entered. It can be understood that each article required the making of a fresh wax model, and the forming with it of a clay mould, and thus every production made by the method varied from the next.

The *cire perdue* process has been in use in different parts of the world for many centuries, has been employed for innumerable articles ranging from statues to vases, and remains in use today for the finest work. Its advantages are that it reproduces faithfully the work of the artist, and that it enables the most complicated shapes to be rendered accurately. It demands great skill from the founder, and from those responsible for the final chiselling.

Less important pieces of simple shapes without any undercutting, for instance horse brasses and furniture mounts, could be cast in fine sand and clay. Bells and mortars were made in a complicated manner employing a combination of this method with that of *cire perdue*.

Another process was that of stamping, for which a patent was obtained in 1769. This involved the use of 'two implements called dies placed under the hammer of a stamp or screw of a press, the one being concave the other convex; which by the pressure of the hammer or screw forced into the die, the shape or the form of the thing designed is accomplished'. The uniform thickness of brass sheets then to be obtained from rolling-mills, and not available by the battery process, together with the greater use of steam-power, led to the spread of stamping. Before very long it had been applied to button-making, then a most important branch of the metal trades, and gradually it spread to other departments of brassware including the manufacture of mounts for furniture.

A metal article was finished in a number of ways: it could be gilded, inlaid, or enamelled. Gilding was usually accomplished in the past by making an amalgam of powdered gold with mercury, coating the piece with it, and placing it in an oven. Heat drove off the mercury, and the remaining gold could be left matt or polished with a burnisher.

Inlaying usually employed gold or silver in bronze, and copper or silver in brass. Often it is known as 'damascening', a name taken from that of the eastern trading-centre, Damascus. The process involved the incising of fine lines in the body of the piece to be decorated, and then metal wires of a contrasting colour were hammered into the incisions.

Enamelling is, in fact, coating the surface of a metal object with a layer of white or coloured glass, or in the case of Canton enamel with a layer of china-stone. There are several methods by which this was accomplished in the case of articles made from copper and from copper alloys. The simplest is that known as *champlevé*: literally, 'flat field', in which the surface is scooped out in places or cast with small hollows, which are then filled with the required colours. In both instances, the colours are in the form of powders which liquefy in the furnace and spread into a mass. This is then ground flat and polished. *Champlevé* enamelling was used in many countries, and an English version dating perhaps to the late seventeenth century is known for some reason as 'Surrey enamel'.

Another enamel process, highly developed in the Far East, is known as *cloisonné*, from the French word, *cloison* for a wall. In this, the surface of the article is decorated with a network of low metal walls soldered to it. The spaces are filled with enamel, and then treated as with *champlevé* but with additional care to avoid melting the solder holding the *cloisons*. The latter, which are very thin, are revealed in the finishing process and gilded.

Finally, all-over enamelling was done by covering completely an article made from very thin copper. If the coating was of white or some other suitable colour the once-baked surface could then be decorated further and baked again. While enamels of this type were made in many countries, those of the Battersea works, on the Thames in London, which were in operation only between 1753 and 1756, have acquired a fame out of proportion to their significance. However, an important process of applying printed decoration to enamels, and subsequently to pottery and porcelain, was introduced there.

CHAPTER TWO

Copper alloys—composition and uses

To most people, brass is a yellow-coloured metal and bronze is a brown one, but the difference between them is more than surface-deep. Primarily, brass is composed of copper and zinc, whereas bronze is an alloy of copper and tin. In each case, varying the proportions of the constituents has the effect of making a different alloy, and the additions of small quantities of other ingredients also affects the ultimate result. The position is additionally confusing to the amateur because not only are some of these alloys very similar to one another in appearance, but several of them are exactly the same in composition and masquerade misleadingly under a number of names.

It is a moot point whether bronze or brass has been the most used of the alloys of copper over the centuries, but as bronze was the first to be invented it must be accorded pride of place

Bronze. There is no strict formula for bronze, any more than there is for the other copper alloys, but in addition to the basic copper it contains a varying proportion of tin. The effect of this is to make the resulting alloy more readily melted and easier to cast into moulds, and at the same time it makes a metal that is harder and less malleable than pure copper.

The alloy was made at least as long ago as 2500 B.C., and the inhabitants of the world at that time were able slowly to perfect their handling of it and use it for purposes in which it has been long supplanted by iron and steel. They were able to harden and sharpen the metal sufficiently to make swords, axes and razors from it, and methods of decoration included ornament that was cut, moulded and, in due course, enamelled. It has been suggested that the invention of bronze was purely accidental; the proximity of copper and tin ores in the earth making this seem highly probable.

Brass. The qualities of brass are varied according to the proportions in which the principal ingredients, copper and zinc, are mixed. In ancient times brass was confused with bronze, and references in the Bible and in ancient documents refer almost certainly to the latter. In the England of Elizabeth I brass was known as Latten, and the differences between the alloys of copper with tin or with zinc were not understood clearly.

Both the strength and the malleability of brass vary according to the formula employed, and the addition of, say, iron improves its performance in certain respects. Brass, according to its composition, was drawn into wire, rolled or hammered into sheets, cast, and stamped.

The following are among some of the many other alloys of copper that have attained popularity at one time or another in the past. Some are still used today, and many of them have been forgotten long ago. Of the latter, mention may be found in old books and in books on collecting, and it may be helpful to know something about them. Some vary only minutely from one another, and a few would seem to be little more than 're-inventions' of earlier alloys.

Argentan. This is an alloy of copper, nickel and zinc, better known under the names of Nickel Silver and German Silver. It has been used as a basis for electro-plating since that process was introduced in 1840, and superseded copper for the purpose. Modern articles are stamped with the letters 'E.P.N.S.', which stand for Electro Plated Nickel Silver.

Bell metal. Used, as implied by its name, for the making of bells. It varied in its proportions of ingredients, copper and tin, from two to one to ten to one, and in both large and small bells other ingredients were sometimes added.

Britannia metal. An alloy used as a substitute for silver, and containing roughly 210 parts of tin to 12 of antimony and 4 of copper. It was invented in the second half of the eighteenth century and first known as White Metal, but by 1797 had acquired the well-known name of Britannia Metal. Many articles made from Britannia Metal after 1840 were electro-plated by Elkington's newly-introduced process, but the plating has worn off subsequently with age and use. Such pieces are purchased sometimes by the unsuspecting as being made of pewter, which it resembles.

Collins metal. Somewhat similar in composition to Keir's Metal (see below), but did not include any iron. It was invented in 1800.

Delta metal. An alloy of copper, zinc and iron which is highly resistant to corrosion. A similar composition is known as **Aich's metal.**

Dutch foil. Silvered copper sheets the thickness of foil, of which pieces are placed behind pastes and other stones in jewellery to increase their effect.

Dutch metal. A brass-like alloy used in the form of very thin leaves as a cheap substitute for gold leaf in the gilding of picture frames, etc.

Muntz's metal. G. F. Muntz (1794–1857) patented in 1832 an alloy of 60 per cent copper and 40 per cent zinc plus a small proportion of iron, which was resistant to the corrosive action of sea-water and suitable for sheathing the wooden hulls of ships. It was manufactured in Birmingham (with a short period in which the business was transferred temporarily to Swansea), and used for many purposes. It was known also as Patent or Yellow metal. G. F. Muntz was a Member of Parliament for Birmingham from 1840 until his death, and may be remembered in that connexion for his part in inducing the government to adopt perforated postage stamps.

Gun metal. A variety of bronze, an alloy of copper and tin varying in proportion according to requirements, developed for the making of gun barrels.

Ormolu. The word means literally 'ground gold' (from the French *or moulu*), and the familiar gilt metal, known in France as *bronze dorée*, is bronze finished with a coating of gold. The cast object is chiselled carefully, then coated with an amalgam of pure gold and mercury, and when this is heated the mercury is given off as a vapour. The gold remains to be burnished where required.

French eighteenth- and nineteenth-century craftsmen were extremely skilled in making all types of articles from ormolu, and these range from chandeliers to mounts for furniture and china. Occasionally, pieces are found stamped with a small crown above a capital 'C', which was a mark used in the manner of a hallmark on silver between 5th March, 1745, and 4th February, 1749. It is suggested that the 'C' stands for *cuivre* (copper), although at one time the view was held that the mark was the initial of one of the famous family of bronze founders named Caffieri.

Ormolu of good quality was made by Matthew Boulton of Birmingham from about 1762, and examples of his workmanship in the form of pairs of candelabra with bodies of Derbyshire Spar (or Blue John, as it is called alternatively) are at Windsor Castle, Saltram in Devonshire, the Victoria and Albert Museum, London, and elsewhere.

German and other continental makers turned their hand to making ormolu during the eighteenth century but, on the whole, their workmanship rarely approached that of the French, and seldom that of the English.

Pinchbeck. It has been said that this is composed of three parts of zinc to four of copper, but whatever its composition the inventor, Christopher Pinchbeck, kept it secret in his lifetime. A clock and watchmaker of eminence until his death in 1732, he was succeeded in business by his son, Edward. In the following year an advertisement in *The Daily Post* announced: 'Notice is hereby given, that the ingenious Mr Edward Pinchbeck, at the Musical Clock, in Fleet Street, does not dispose of one grain of his curious metal, which so nearly resembles gold in colour, smell, and ductility, to any person whatsoever; nor are the toys made of the said metal sold by any one person in England except himself.' It should be mentioned that in the eighteenth century the word Toy was used to describe any trifling article, such as a seal or a snuff-box, and was not restricted to children's playthings. Many small objects made from Pinchbeck still survive, and the term remains current in the English language for anything spurious or sham.

Keir's metal. James Keir, a Scotsman, was born in 1735, and after a career in the army manufactured glass at Stourbridge, near Birmingham. In 1779 he patented an alloy of his invention, comprising '100 parts of copper, 75 of zinc or spelter and 10 of iron', specifically for making sheathing and nails for ships. Matthew Boulton encouraged him to exploit it, but a test made by the Admiralty was not a success and it appears that no further action was taken in this direction. Later, Keir opened a factory at Tipton, Staffordshire, and there made metal-framed windows which were supplied to 'many principal mansions in the kingdom', including, it is said, Windsor Castle and Carlton House.

Paktong. An alloy of copper, zinc and nickel which polishes to resemble silver and resists tarnish. It was imported into England from China in the eighteenth century, and used to make candlesticks, grates, fenders, and other articles. For some reason it was confused with Tutenag, pure zinc from the same country, and old writers speak of objects as being made from the latter when meaning Paktong.

Prince's metal. This metal, a type of brass, was the invention of Prince Rupert of Bavaria (1619–1682), son of Elizabeth, the daughter of King James I of England. After spending his early years in Holland, he came to England in 1642 to assist his uncle, Charles I, and led his army in the Civil War. Not only did he invent the metal bearing his name, but he experimented in such diverse subjects as mezzotint-engraving, gun-founding and the making of gunpowder. In January 1690 John Hervey, later first Earl of Bristol, noted in his diary: 'Paid for six dozen of Princes metal buttons, £1 10s.'

Speculum. Known sometimes as Steel, this alloy was used from ancient times for the making of mirrors, as it is durable and takes a high polish of a silvery colour. A recipe for making Speculum, printed in a book issued in 1701, reads as follows: 'Refined copper 3 lbs., melt it, then add of fine tin 9 lbs.; as soon as they are melted add red tartar calcined 18 ozs., white arsenic 6 ozs., nitre 3 ozs., alum 1 ounce, keep these in a melting heat for 3 or 4 hours that the salts may evaporate; then cast it into moulds.' Polishing the rough-surfaced cast metal was a laborious task, involving grinding carefully with a sequence of stones of lessening coarseness, and finally with tin dross. A final word of advice, given at the same time, relates to everday cleaning: 'If these glasses are sullied or made dull with the air or any thick vapour, you must clear them by rubbing, not with woollen or linen, but with a piece of deer or goat skin, wiping it in an oblique line.'

While Speculum was used for making hand and wall mirrors during many centuries, long after it had been replaced by glass for this purpose it was still employed for reflecting mirrors in telescopes and other scientific instruments.

Other names current at various dates for alloys of copper are **Bath metal, Mannheim gold, Mosaic gold, Similor,** and **Tombac.**

Japanese alloys include **Shaduko**, three parts of gold to ninety-seven of copper, and **Shibuichi**, with one part of silver to three of copper. With both of these, as with pure copper and with iron, the Japanese metalworkers rely for effect on the final treatment for patination after the articles have been cast and chased or hammered. Shaduko becomes finally a velvety black, and Shibuichi can attain a number of shades of grey.

In the north of India an alloy named **Ashtadhatu** was made from a mixture of copper, lead, zinc, tin, iron, mercury, silver and gold, and elsewhere use was made of an alloy called **Panchalouha.** This was composed of copper, brass and white lead with an occasional addition of silver and gold.

It should be stressed that where proportions of ingredients have been given they are no more than approximate. Each individual craftsman had his secrets, and every single 'mix' must have varied, even if by only a minute amount, and affected the finished product. This applies to both European and Eastern alloys.

CHAPTER THREE

Countries in which used

THE following pages provide some very brief notes on many of the lands in which copper alloys have been used in the past, and an indication of the types of articles in which craftsmen of each country specialized.

It remains uncertain whether the Chinese, the Egyptians or some other Far or Near Eastern race was the first to use bronze. Sometime between 3,000 and 2,000 B.C. the inhabitants of the island of Crete were prominent in their use of it, and travelled far and wide in search of tin and copper. The Phoenicians also took up the search, and are said to have founded Cadiz in Spain as a convenient depot, and from there it has been assumed that they reached Cornwall, in the south-west of England.

The peak of skill in metalworking in early times was reached by the Assyrians and the Greeks; the former being recorded as having armoured the walls of some of their cities with sheets of bronze. The Greek sculptor Phidias made huge statues from shaped panels of bronze riveted together; a process of manufacture superseded eventually by casting. Ancient Greek bronzes have survived the centuries, and show the great artistry of their craftsmen. Not only was bronze used alone, but its effect was sometimes heightened in portrayals of the human head by inlays of gold or silver for the lips and eyes.

The Romans made great use of bronze in imitation of the Greeks, and by about 20 B.C. had coins of brass. This metal they used also for the making of brooches and other personal ornaments.

Celtic art, simple and altogether less sophisticated than that to be found by the Mediterranean, was based in the main on variations of scrolls, circles, and geometric forms.

It reached a high state of development in the settlement of La Tène, by the Lake of Neuchâtel in Switzerland, where large finds of metalwork bearing Celtic ornament have been discovered. From there it reached France and the British Isles; the latter prior to the Roman Invasion. Celtic forms endured for longer in Ireland and Scotland than in England, where they were displaced by the introductions of the invaders.

Africa. The most important group of copper or bronze works from the continent of Africa are those produced in the Benin region of Nigeria. It is thought that the tribe in this area, the Bini, learned their art from the neighbouring Yoruba at Ife, but the date when this came about is uncertain; as early as the thirteenth century has been suggested by one authority. Benin metalwork was virtually unknown in Europe until a party of Englishmen was massacred while on their way to Benin City in 1897, and a punitive expedition captured the city. Great quantities of locally-made bronze and other objects were then discovered and brought to the west.

The Bini employed the *cire perdue* process for casting and were highly skilled in its use. Articles of many kinds were made, and prominent amongst them is a series of finely-modelled human heads. A large number of plaques modelled with historical and mythological scenes were found also, and there are representative collections of these, and other pieces, at the British Museum in London, and elsewhere.

The other African tribe noted for their metalwork is the Ashanti, inhabitants of a district of the former Gold Coast, now Ghana. Again, use was made of the *cire perdue* method, and this was employed principally for making small weights and boxes for gold dust. Of the former it has been written: 'much imagination is required in order to find major aesthetic value in them'.

America. The indigenous Indians knew of copper and used it on a small scale, but it was not until the eighteenth century and the colonization of the country with Europeans was well under way, that metal wares began to be produced in any quantity. 'John Halden, Brasier from London, near the Old-Slip-Market in New York' advertised in 1744 that he made and sold articles of copper and brass, and also that he 'gives Ready Money for old Copper, Brass, Pewter or Lead'; from the latter it may be inferred that he made old pots into new, and not all his stock was imported from England. Between 1762 and 1771 another brazier, James Byers, announced that he made andirons, candlesticks, etc., and cast brass pump chambers and mill parts. As an afterthought he mentioned that he 'also makes Wire Cages for parrots'.

While there were a number of practical brass and copper workers established by the middle of the century, none of their work has been identified. Doubtless they copied European originals, from which their products are now indistinguishable. A number of copper warming-pans are known to have been made by Charles Hunneman, a coppersmith of Boston, and others bear stamped initials; unfortunately, the latter remain a mystery and we do not yet know to whom they belonged.

In the nineteenth century, with the rapid spread of mechanization, new processes made it possible to make copper and brass articles in great quantities, many of them stamped with the name of their maker. Such pieces, of course, are much less rare than those of earlier date, but at least they can be identified without doubt and they are being collected in the United States today.

Belgium. The town of Dinant on the River Meuse was famous as a centre for the manufacture of brass wares from about the tenth century A.D. Copper was obtained for the purpose from German merchants who brought it from the great mines in the Harz mountains, and from Scandinavia. Calamine, from which zinc is extracted, was found on the spot. For this reason, brass was made instead of bronze; an alloy used almost everywhere else. The finished articles were exported far and wide, and Mosan brass (*Mosan:* so-called because it came from the district by the River Meuse) enjoyed a big reputation. Alternatively, it is known from the name of the principal town of the area, Dinant, as Dinanderie.

Probably the most celebrated and important wares were those made for the numerous cathedrals and churches on the Continent. A typical example is the large bronze font made early in the twelfth century for the cathedral of St Lambert, Liége, and when this building was destroyed in the Revolution removed to the church of St Barthélemy in the same city. The bowl stands on the backs of ten oxen, each with its head in a different position, and round it are five groups of baptismal scenes modelled in high relief.

In the church of Nôtre Dame at Tongres, a few miles to the north of Liége, is a brass eagle lectern and a Paschal candlestick, the latter standing 10 ft. in height; both bear inscriptions showing they were made at Dinant, and the candlestick is dated 1460-62. However, these and a few other pieces are quite exceptional, and the majority of the productions of the district was of smaller articles for general use. These included such things as aquamaniles, candlesticks, cooking-pots and other domestic wares of which examples must surely survive, but cannot now be identified with certainty as coming from the region.

Philippe le Bon, Duke of Burgundy, captured and sacked Dinant in 1466, and many of the brassworkers then left the town to find a haven elsewhere in the region and farther afield. However, as late as 1746 it was recorded of Dinant that 'it is a place of some trade, particularly in manufactures of brass and iron'.

China. Copper and its alloys have been known and used in China for several thousand years. The great mines in Yunnan province, an independent state subdued by Kublai Khan in the thirteenth century but not incorporated in the

Chinese Empire until 400 years later, supplied not only most of the needs of China, but also Burma. In 1697 further mines were started in the Tungshan Hills, north of Nankin, and in 1738 became a government monopoly. By the end of the century Chinese mines had reached an output of some 8,000 tons a year.

Zinc was found principally in Yunnan, and much of this was exported at various dates to Holland and Germany. A certain amount reached England, where it was known commercially as Tutenag, and some ingots have been found in Kuantung which assayed as 98 per cent pure and bear the date 1585. An alloy of copper, zinc and nickel, named Paktong, was exported also, but in England the name of this hard metal became confused somehow with that of the pure zinc. Articles made from Paktong, which has a silvery appearance and resists tarnish, were and still are referred to commonly as Tutenag.

Rarely was copper, *ch'e-chin* or red metal, employed on its own, in most instances it was alloyed with tin. The *K'ao kung chi*, a work attributed to the Chou dynasty (1122–249 B.C.) and dealing with the industries of the time, lists six of the alloys in current use. They are as follows:

1. Five parts of copper and one part of tin: for making bells, gongs, cauldrons, sacrificial vases and vessels, and measures.
2. Four parts of copper and one of tin: for axes and hatchets.
3. Three parts of copper and one of tin: for halberds and spears.
4. Two parts of copper and one of tin: for swords and agricultural implements.
5. Three parts of copper and two of tin: for arrow-heads used in hunting and in war, for curved and pointed knives for incising inscriptions on bamboo, and 'for scraping the surface of the wooden tables on which the

COPPER AND ITS ALLOYS

characters were written with a wooden style dipped in varnish'.

6 One part of copper and one of tin: for mirrors, both flat and concave.

Much information about ancient Chinese bronzes is to be found in the *Illustrated Description of the Palace Antiquities* (*Hsüan Ho Po Ku T'ou Lu*) a thirty-volume record written by Wang Fu early in the twelfth century, and in other descriptions of collections compiled by Lü Ta-Lin in the year A.D. 1092. Other catalogues of the Imperial collections of bronzes were made in the mid-eighteenth century, and these and others have been reproduced in modern times. From a study of these important old documents, and the surviving authentic examples of the wares themselves, much has been learned in both East and West about the different styles of design and ornament current during successive periods.

All the Chinese bronzes were made by the *cire perdue* method, and carefully finished afterwards. Most of the older pieces have been excavated, and, the soil of China is such that most unusual colour effects have resulted with the passing of time; a process that has been aided by impurities in the tin forming part of the composition. While this was doubtless the purest obtainable, it had in it traceable quantities of lead and zinc.

The respect accorded in the past to bronze in China is reflected in the fact that the forms in which it was made were copied in pottery, porcelain and jade. Not only were the shapes copied in those materials, but attempts were made to simulate the colours. Later, the shapes persisted, and it is not unusual to find an eighteenth century K'ang Hsi piece of clearly recognizable bronze shape, but decorated inappropriately in the colours of the *famille verte*.

Surviving ancient bronzes take a number of forms, and these include the following:

Ting. A three-or four-legged cooking vessel, the body either circular or rectangular, and sometimes provided with a cover.

Kuei. A bowl for containing food, sometimes with a cover.

Chung. A bell.

Hu, Ku and Yu. Types of wine vessels, some with covers and others without.

Chuo. A sacrificial, or libation, cup.

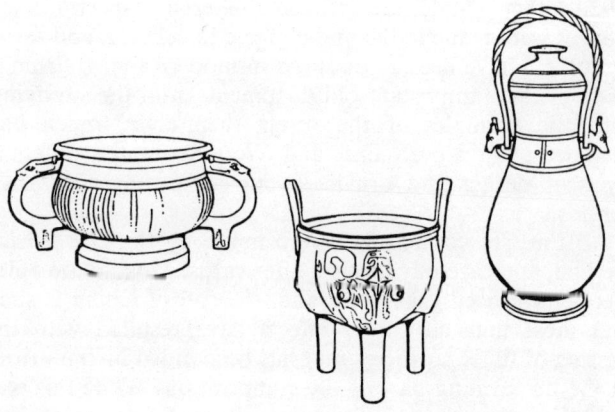

Figure 1. (l. to r.) Kuei, Ting and Yu.

Most pieces rely on their shape and on moulded and chiselled ornament for their effectiveness, but from early times some were inlaid with patterns in gold and silver.

General shaping as well as details of ornament changed with each period, but there are often styles that overlapped in time and are difficult to place satisfactorily in any of the accepted categories. The various compilers of the Chinese catalogues arranged the pieces they described in different ways: either according to the intended use of each item, or according to the assumed age. The last being open to criticism in view of the fact that the earliest of the catalogues recorded pieces that had been made as much as 2,000 years earlier. Various modern authorities have proposed fresh systems of grouping. In 1933 the then Crown Prince of Sweden, now H.M. the King of Sweden, supported a proposal for a series of five stylistic divisions. Two years later, the Chinese Government, which lent 108 fine bronzes to the exhibition of Chinese Art held in London in 1935/6, divided them into six groups. Professor E. Perceval Yetts, in the Introduction to the catalogue of another important London exhibition, that of Early Chinese Bronzes, organized by the Oriental Ceramic Society in 1951, used what he termed the 'Three Phases'. These were described as: 'The First Phase includes bronzes displaying the standards established in the Shang-Yin period, and it lasted from earliest times to the tenth century B.C. The Second Phase includes the style distinctive of Chou culture, and it lasted from the tenth century to dates which varied in different parts of the country. The Third Phase corresponds generally to what is known as Ch'in or Huai style.'

The later Chinese bronzes, which imitate the appearance of archaic examples, are fairly plentiful and cheap. Although they copy the shapes and decoration of early pieces they do not often attempt to simulate the patina, and cannot be considered seriously as dangerous fakes. A quantity of bronzes do fall into this latter category, and with these the forger has tried hard to imitate the green hues that are the attractive feature, and partly the guarantee of age, of genuine specimens. The patina is copied sometimes by a liberal application of wax or paint, or more effectively by prolonged immersion in a cess-pit. In view of the high value of an undoubtedly genuine example, such faking can be a worth-while proposition—although not for the collector.

Some Chinese connoisseurs remove the crust of patina from an old bronze, as they prefer to see the pure metal and any delicate decoration it may bear, but examples that have been treated in this manner seldom appeal to European collectors. A further problem arises when a modern patina replaces an old one that has been removed from a bronze that is basically quite genuine.

The dating of *cloisonné* enamels, which range from the fifteenth century onwards, is not dissimilar to that of bronzes. Again, it will be found that the styles overlapped throughout and only general groupings are possible until more knowledge has been gained. The most popular examples of the technique are probably the figures of birds and animals; quails, storks, ducks and deer are among those that were made, mostly during the eighteenth century and later.

Large quantities of vases, bowls and other pieces were decorated in *cloisonné* enamel, but only rarely are the most important examples on the market in the West. The most noteworthy specimens were made in the short reign of Ching-t'ai (1450–56), so much so that in later years the term 'Ching-t'ai' was given to *cloisonné* in general and the mark of the period was applied indiscriminately. Pieces older than the eighteenth century command high prices, but for each old specimen there are several hundred of more modern manufacture. Many that have been imported from the Far East during the past thirty or forty years have been given, or have acquired, a look of apparent age, and it is customary for them to be accepted by the ignorant and the unscrupulous as being far older than they really are.

Early in the eighteenth century a factory was started in Pekin to make enamels on copper: articles formed from thin sheets of the metal were covered in powdered china-stone, fired and then decorated. This process was in imitation of European enamels introduced into China by French Jesuit missionaries at the capital, and eventually the manufacture centred on Canton which gave its name to the ware. Canton Enamel was (and still is) made almost exclusively for the export market, and many of the older pieces bear decoration in the form of paintings of European subjects in *famille rose* colours. Some examples have the mark of the reign of Ch'ien Lung (1735–95). Modern pieces are roughly made and poorly painted when compared with old examples, and an examination of old and new side by side will prove instructive.

France. Following the working of metals from ancient times, the thirteenth century saw the rise to prominence of the craftsmen of Limoges, a town to the south-west of Paris. They specialized in the making of articles of copper or bronze decorated with enamels. At first this was done by cutting or moulding small areas which were then filled with colours, but was followed by the process of covering the article completely with enamel and subsequently painting it. Among the known artists who worked in the latter manner at Limoges is the Limousin family, especially Léonard who lived from 1505 to 1577, Nardon Pénicaud, and Pierre Raymond.

The great majority of the earliest French copper and bronze was destroyed long ago. The many wars that ravaged Europe successively were responsible for the conversion of works-of-art of all countries into cannon and shot and finally, in France, the Revolution completed the toll. Limoges enamels were included among the medieval objects in which great interest was shown in the mid-nineteenth century. In addition to research into the history and origins of the various productions, an abundant crop of copies was made. After a century or more of wear-and-tear these often show deceptive indications of apparent age; they show, also, few of the signs of careful workmanship that a study of genuine examples will reveal to the collector.

The introduction of gilt bronze (ormolu) took place in the late seventeenth century. Its use as mounts on furniture, for chandeliers and wall-lights, for mounting porcelain, and for many other purposes, is so characteristically French that much work made elsewhere is automatically labelled as made in that country. Although the rococo designs of the early and mid-eighteenth century are probably the most striking, the workmanship during the reign of Louis XVI (1774–92) is unequalled. There are many fine examples of ormolu to be seen in London, in the Jones Collection in the Victoria and Albert Museum and in the Wallace Collection, Manchester Square, but there is little in the provinces (an exception is the Rothschild Collection at Waddesdon Manor, Hertfordshire, a National Trust property). In France, of course, its distribution is more widespread, but on the whole the finest is to be seen in Paris.

French eighteenth-century ormolu is expensive, and a genuine pair of Louis XV wall-lights has fetched as much as £1,300 at auction in London in recent years. There is no shortage of less-expensive specimens of later date but in the manner of the old, which are sometimes confusingly similar to both expert and amateur.

Germany. In the tenth and eleventh centuries the German bronze workers rivalled those of Italy, and under the influence of Bernward, Bishop of Hildesheim from 993 to 1022, many masterpieces were produced. The city is at the north foot of the Harz mountains, famous for minerals including copper, and a few miles from Hanover. Still to be seen at the cathedral are the great bronze doors, a 15 ft. high column modelled in relief with scenes from the life of Christ, and two fine altar candlesticks; all dating from the time of Bernward. Augsburg and Nuremburg were also important centres of metal-working, and at the latter city the most celebrated bronze-maker was Hermann Vischer, succeeded by his son Peter (1455 to 1529), and by his grandsons. These men and others, made fine bronze statuettes in the Italian manner. They have not received the wide attention given to those from Italy, but they are probably rarer and equally worthy of study.

Among the attractive pieces made in the fifteenth century, and of which specimens have survived, are some gilt copper cups and covers modelled as baronial strongholds. One of these, in the Victoria and Albert Museum, standing $14\frac{1}{2}$ in. high, is complete with chapel, water-mill and steepled castle. Even the supports are in the form of miniature turreted castles, and the whole piece has a fairylike appearance as though some of the Grimm brothers' characters might well inhabit it. Such pieces are of course rare now, and it is still uncertain whether they were made originally as samples of skilled workmanship, or for purchase by those unable to afford the cost of similar cups in real gold or silver-gilt.

More practical in appearance and purpose are the copper and brass tobacco-boxes produced in quantity in the second half of the eighteenth century at the metalworking town of Iserlohn, near Dortmund.

Great Britain. The first use of metal in the British Isles dates perhaps from about 2000 B.C.: bronze axes, daggers, spearheads, and other objects have been excavated that were made in what is termed the Early Bronze Age, which lasted until 1400 B.C. Two axe-heads found in Co. Sligo, Eire, are not only decorated with bands of ornament but bear distinct traces of having been cast in two-piece moulds. In the British Museum and elsewhere are moulds cut in stone and used for casting such articles; they have been excavated in places as far apart as Co. Durham in the north of England, Helsbury Quarry, Michaelstow, Cornwall, in the far west, and Lough Gur, Co. Limerick, Eire. Also at the British Museum is a set of bronzesmith's tools, again from Eire, including hammers, chisels, a gouge and an anvil.

The Middle Bronze Age (1400 to 1000 B.C.) covers the transition to the Late Bronze Age (1000 to 350 B.C.) when more definite changes can be noticed. It is marked by a great increase in the use of metal, and an extension of the types of articles made from it. Hitherto confined mainly to weapons and tools, this wider use embraced trumpets, cauldrons and shields. Axes and spear heads continued to be made, and their design resulted in greater effectiveness in use as well as an increase in decoration. Both were made with socketed heads and were no longer tied to a handle with leather thonging, and the sword acquired an improved shape.

In many instances, metal and other excavated articles can be dated with more accuracy than their origins can be decided. As in later periods, succeeding waves of foreign workers settled in the isles and brought with them their own native designs and methods of manufacture. These were assimilated quickly by local workers, and it becomes very difficult to distinguish imported work from that done by residents. Many objects of decidedly Scandinavian form found in the east of England, and of French, German and Iberian types found in the south and west, may equally have been brought by immigrants or invaders, or have been made by craftsmen of those nationalities who settled on English soil.

While a number of articles of copper and its alloys dating from medieval times survive in England, again it is not always possible to say positively whether they were made actually in this country or to the order of English merchants abroad. In many instances it is highly probable that the question can never be answered satisfactorily, but it is a query that applies in almost the complete range of manufactured goods down the ages. It is met with even at the present day, but is simplified by the fact that most countries now require imports to bear on them the name of the country of origin.

As it is, pieces made in the past must be judged mainly on their appearance: decoration when present, quality of finish, and identifiable and datable markings and coats-of-arms or names. For instance, there is every reason for assuming as of English manufacture some jugs dating from the second half of the fourteenth century. One of these in the British Museum, stands 21 in. in height and is cast with two couplets in raised letters, which read:

> '*He that will not spare when he may*
> *He shall not spend when he would*',

and

> '*Deem the best in every doubt*
> *Till the truth be tried out*'.

In addition, it shows the arms of England as borne in the reign of Richard II, who died in the year 1400.

An Anglo-German partnership in mines at Keswick, Cumberland, resulted in the formation of the Company of Mines Royal in 1568, and in about the same year the Society of the Mineral and Battery Works came into being. Both were smiled upon by Monarch and Parliament and enjoyed some years of success, but in spite of amalgamation in 1668 their monopoly resulted in stagnation. Only after 1693, when an Act freed the mines for development by private enterprise, did mining begin in earnest. During the seventeenth century, much brass had been imported ready alloyed from Holland and Germany, and copper from Sweden; the latter country having ample supplies of timber for use in smelting. Following the freeing of the mines from monopoly came the discovery that the ore might be smelted successfully with coal. The result of this was the establishment of the South Wales smelting industry: well situated for transport of the ore and for abundant coal.

There was a further invasion of foreign workers following the revocation of the Edict of Nantes in 1685; which led to the prosecution of Protestants in France and their hurried flight from the country. Craftsmen of all kinds came to the British Isles, and these included workers in copper and its alloys. Again, the immigrants brought with them fresh ideas and taught them to the workers already in the land in which they settled, but again, in this period, it is nearly impossible to tell in which country much of the work was done.

Probably the most popular metal article made between the years 1600 and 1800 was the candlestick, and the various designs of this executed in England came in the first instance from countries on the mainland of Europe. These were duly modified by the English craftsmen to suit his own taste and that of his clients, and resulted on the whole in a simplification of form. On the other hand, it has been assumed very often that where two similar articles are concerned, the plainer is the English one. This is not always the case, and such an over-clarification is not a reliable guide. It is accepted, however, that candlesticks with a small hole near the top of the holder and to one side are of Dutch origin; and that English ones, alike in almost every other respect, do not have this significant hole. It was provided for the purpose of inserting a pointed instrument to remove the butt of a candle; it seems a sensible idea and we may wonder why it was not used in the British Isles.

The metal trades in England centred on Birmingham at least as early as the sixteenth century, when in 1538 John Leland wrote of smiths and cutlers being there. Both these trades eventually left the town, and were replaced by a multiplicity of others relying on copper and its alloys. The peak was reached in about 1760, when Matthew Boulton established and built his Soho works, and spread the fame of his name and that of his country throughout the world.

Boulton was born in 1728. He made not only brasswares of every kind, including ormolu of fine quality, but minted coins and medals and supplied machinery for the purpose to the Royal Mint in London and to Russia, Spain and Denmark. All his productions are distinguished by the care that was taken in both their design and their manufacture, and his output was of a high standard in every department. One of his noteworthy ventures was to form a partnership with James Watt to manufacture the steam-engines invented and designed by the latter.

In 1768, copper was re-discovered in Wales; the vast deposits lying close to the surface at Parys Mountain, Anglesey, which had been worked originally by the Romans.

COPPER AND ITS ALLOYS

The ease with which this could be removed offset the fact that it was not of such high quality as the Cornish ore, and the further point in its favour that it was comparatively close to the big smelting works dealt a big blow to the miners in Cornwall. The increase in supplies caused a glut of copper on the market, and the Cornish had to seek ways of reducing their costs, or close down. To get more ore meant sinking the mines deeper, and pumping water from them at depths that had not hitherto been necessary or possible. In 1776 the Cornish started negotiations with James Watt, and by 1780 there were forty of his engines at work in the county. Within ten years demand had increased, the glut was a shortage, and Boulton was anxiously trying to buy copper to carry on his manufactory at Soho.

One of the important advances in metalworking was the introduction of the process of stamping articles in quantity from sheet metal, which was particularly successful with brass. It was the subject of a patent in 1769, obtained by John Pickering of London, but full use was not made of the idea until the wider use of steam made a convenient source of power readily available. Not only could greatly increased quantities of goods be made within a given time, but far less metal was used than in casting and expense was saved in two directions.

Copper was used extensively in ship-building from the middle years of the eighteenth century. The wooden vessels of the time, both naval and civil, were prone to attacks by a sea creature, the Ship Worm; a destructive mollusc of the genus *Teredos*. It was found that if vessels had their bottoms sheathed in copper, trouble of this nature was prevented, and the saving of the hull offset the cost of the extra material and labour. The first use of this antidote was reported in the *Gentleman's Magazine* in 1761, in a paragraph reading as follows:

'The sheathing of the *Alarm* frigate of 52 guns was

finished. It is of copper, the first that ever was made of this kind of sheathing; it is very neat, not heavy, nor very expensive. She is designed for the West Indies.'

Experiments continued in efforts to find cheaper and effective substitutes. As late as 1832 G. F. Muntz patented an alloy which was given his own name, and was devised primarily for ships' bottoms. It was used with success for that purpose, but not less for others, until finally the iron hull did away with the need for sheathing.

The invention of the process called Sheffield-plating led to a further big consumption of copper. Thomas Bolsover of Sheffield had found in 1742 that sheets of silver and copper could be fused together and then treated as though they were one metal, but it was not until about sixteen years later that the process began to be used on any scale. Plated ware was produced by many manufacturers in the Sheffield area, and not least by Boulton of Birmingham. Great numbers of pieces were made, exactly resembling solid silver but costing only a fraction compared with the price of the articles they imitated so closely. Not only was copper cheaper than silver, but articles made from the latter paid a government tax and plated wares were free of duty. Sheffield plate continued to be made with a basis of pure copper, until alloys replaced it in about 1830. These were Nickel silver, German silver, or Argentan, and before long the process of depositing silver on one of these by electrical methods, known as electro-plating, entirely superseded Sheffield plate.

In about 1830 there was a general revival of interest in England in old forms of art, and many books appeared on the subject. Augustus Welby Pugin (1812–52), an architect with a consuming passion for everything Gothic, became leader of the movement. His books, illustrated with his own engravings, and his work at Alton Towers for the Earl of Shrewsbury and the design of St Chad's at Birmingham, led the way to his provision of a Medieval Court in the 1851 Great Exhibition. The Court contained a display of ecclesiastical furniture and fittings in the Gothic manner: the latter including 'brass lecterns, with book-desks, and figures of various kinds; Altar with brass pillars, and other appurtenances, in the old French style; Candlesticks, with various ornamental figures, in antique style.' The articles shown on that occasion influenced taste, both in and out of the Church, for much of the remainder of the century. They stimulated a wide interest in the antique and were responsible for a considerable amount of close copying of medieval originals, both by those unable to create original designs in the popular taste and by others who sought to deceive deliberately collectors of the genuinely old.

Holland. The flight of craftsmen from the Dinant district of Belgium after the capture of the city in 1466, undoubtedly drove many of them to take refuge in Holland. It is probable, however, that the work done there by the immigrants cannot be distinguished now from that done elsewhere. Unquestionably, by the sixteenth century there were casters of bells and mortars working in the Netherlands, and this is proved by extant specimens moulded with their names and the date when the work was done. Dutch and Belgian mortars have been the subject of much research in Holland; even when they are unsigned it is often possible to date them and allocate them to a specific maker by means of published lists of decoration found on signed examples.

From the seventeenth century onwards much copper and brass ware was exported from Holland, especially to England. Some of this originated in northern Belgium and the rest came from Holland and Germany. With the nineteenth-century revival of interest in the age of Elizabeth I and the medieval period in history even more was sent over, to go with 'Tudor' oak from the same sources. As with the furniture, some of the metalwork masquerades still as being of English make. On the whole, the subject has received little study, perhaps because so much of the copper and brass ware lacks merit.

India and neighbouring countries. Copper and its alloys were used widely from about the seventh century A.D. for making images of the innumerable deities of Buddhism. The figures vary in design from Ganesha, distinguished by his elephant's head, to the graceful Parvati who is depicted as a beautiful woman posed gracefully, but in some instances with a double complement of heads, arms and hands. The number of different figures runs to some hundreds, making their identification difficult, and variations in belief over the centuries add to the complexity. Whereas rules were laid down long ago for the help of modellers, detailing the relative proportions of the parts of the human body and the different postures in which it should be portrayed, the various attributes of the images often resemble one another closely and cause confusion. In the words of a recent writer: 'Figures have been excavated or discovered where no two experts have agreed on their identification, each having plausible reasons for his dissent'; which may or may not encourage the beginner.

For public display the figures were carried in procession on litters, and for this purpose were made sometimes with holes in their bases so that they could be tied securely. Many of them have two short posts at the back corners instead of a metal arch (known as a *prabha*), which is present in some cases. The posts were to hold an arch of flowers, giving a more attractive appearance than the metal and lessening the weight considerably.

All these Indian figures were cast by the *cire perdue* method, and consequently each differs more or less from the other. Over the centuries the designs of individual images have altered slightly, but the changes are minor in view of the length of time involved. Many of the earlier examples show faces with heavy eye-lids and noticeably full lips, but such specimens are rare. Accurate dating is often a matter for

COPPER AND ITS ALLOYS

argument, and equally difficult in some instances is the exact district of origin.

Similar figures of gods and goddesses, but with local differences in their features, attributes and minor decoration, were made also in Ceylon, Java, Cambodia and Tibet. While many were bronzed, a proportion were finished with gilding, and some were inlaid with turquoise and coral. The Tibetans made also well-designed sacrificial bowls, prayer-wheels and other articles for use in connexion with religious observances. These latter include macabre cups made from human skulls mounted in gilt bronze set with gems, and used also in temples. Of secular objects the elaborately modelled teapots of bronze are distinctive. Many bronzes, especially figures of Buddhist gods and goddesses were made to Tibetan order in both Nepal and China, and it is not easy to distinguish them from those made in Tibet itself. It is said that the decorative flower-like *motif* incised on the removable plate under the base of a figure, in which inscribed papers are placed when the bronze is dedicated, varies in design between the different countries of origin. As the small plate is often missing this suggested aid to identification is of doubtful help and, in any case, is not an infallible guide.

Brass and copper were used very widely in India for making articles other than figures, and many pieces were ornamented elaborately with damascening in silver or gold. The so-called *Bidri* work, owing its name to the town of Bihar to the north of Hyderabad, is inlaid with silver in an alloy of copper, lead, tin and zinc; with the latter preponderating. The ground is treated with chemicals that stain it black in contrast to the polished silver patterns shining against it.

Other styles of inlaying include those in which the engraved brass ground is filled with red, green or black lacquer. A further method is for either copper or brass articles to be tinned all over before the thin coating of tin is cut through in a pattern to expose the basic metal. These and other local styles were revived extensively in the later years of the nineteenth century, and some of the wares were copied in England to be exported to India. Not a few of these pieces returned to the country of their origin as 'genuine native work'. Indian pieces of early date are noticeable for their careful execution and are rare, but the majority of surviving Indian or pseudo-Indian brass and copper wares are little more than eighty years old, and most are considerably less.

Iran. While numerous types of bronzes were made in ancient Persia, modern interest has been directed in particular to those from Luristan in the north-west of the country. Horse-bits and other small portable objects for everyday use were made apparently by a local tribe, and are marked in their design by a most distinctive and imaginative treatment of human and animal motives.

Islam. The spread of the Mohammedan religion and the sweeping victories of its adherents resulted in the Arab world extending, at one period, from the borders of China to the shores of the Atlantic in Spain. It embraced the cultures of Syria, Iran, Egypt and Iraq, and included, among others of importance, the cities of Damascus, Bagdad, Cairo and Granada. While each of the overrun nations did to some extent retain the individuality of its arts, the influence of a common religion overspread them all. The word Islam is an Arabic one meaning in effect, 'pious submission to the word of God', and is used to describe conveniently all those people who adopted the teaching of Mohammed of Mecca.

Mohammed was born about A.D. 570, and the art of decorating cast and beaten metal with engraving and inlaying was then well known to many of the Arab tribes, but little survives from that time. Examples excavated at Hamadan, in western Iran, comprise bronze vessels engraved with elaborate patterns made during the twelfth and thirteenth centuries. Of the latter date there have been preserved a number of finely inlaid and engraved brass ewers, of which a typical specimen is in the Victoria and Albert Museum, London. It is inlaid in a complex pattern of so-called 'arabesque' (Arab-style) ornament; birds, and human figures in engraved silver on a ground of black pigment. Another, in the Metropolitan Museum, New York, shows musicians performing and men filling wine-cups from a vat, and bears an inscription stating that it was made in the year 1226/7.

The last-named piece was the work of an Iraq metalworker but pieces of closely-similar design were made elsewhere, especially at Cairo and Damascus. Unless they are inscribed or show strong local characteristics it is almost impossible to be certain exactly where they originated.

Brass and copper articles, some inlaid with engraved silver and copper, have been made continuously in one Islamic country or another. Examples of later date than those mentioned above are often in the same styles as early ones, and differ only in their less accomplished craftsmanship. Whereas old specimens are very rare and consequently valuable, modern versions are commonplace and should be inexpensive.

Italy. The Italians acquired their skill in bronze-making from the Greeks, and workers from Byzantium were responsible for making some of the magnificent doors still to be seen outside Italian cathedrals and churches. In time, the Italians learned the art and soon they, in turn, inspired others and knowledge spread throughout Europe. Apart from these doors and other achievements on a large scale which continued to be made, Italy is renowned above all for large numbers of small-sized bronzes, many purely decorative but others utilitarian, made in the fifteenth and sixteenth centuries.

Many of these pieces were inspired by, or adapted from, antique originals, and this cult of the ancient reached its zenith when incomplete figures, in close imitation of excavated fragments, were made deliberately. Probably the most popular of the bronzes, judged by the numbers extant, were the inkstands and other pieces by Andrea Briosco, known as Riccio ('Curley-head') each of which is ornamented usually with a male or a female satyr. Other characteristic specimens were a speciality of Paduan workers, who were famous for their life-like figures of animals. These include toads, snakes and crabs, and their realism is partly due to the fact that they were made from casts of actual specimens.

Prominent in the late sixteenth century was the sculptor Giovanni Bologna, born at Douai in Flanders in 1524, who spent all his working life at Florence where he died in 1608. Many copies of his marble groups were reproduced on a small scale in bronze. Not only were they made in the sculptor's studio and under his immediate supervision, but they have been imitated elsewhere from shortly after his death until the present day. Bologna excelled in groups and figures, which were well modelled and often represented mythological subjects, and his men and women usually display vigorous action.

The smaller bronzes have been studied closely, and many of the surviving examples are the work of the most talented artists of their time. Their high artistic and technical significance has long been recognized, and only the briefest outline of their great importance has been attempted here. Finally, it should be remembered that the high commercial value of Italian bronzes over the past fifty years and more has made faking worth while.

Japan. Probably the first Japanese metal objects to reach Europe were the corners, hinges and lock-plates on lacquered wood cabinets imported during the seventeenth century. They were made of copper, incised with patterns and finished with gilding; quite unlike anything of the kind then current in the West. Little else of metal was exported from Japan until the country was opened up for general

COPPER AND ITS ALLOYS

trading at the end of the nineteenth century, and then a great flood of metal wares reached Europe and America; a flood that has continued to flow, on a diminishing scale as regards both quantity and quality, ever since.

Earlier, however, the Japanese had become highly proficient in the making of all kinds of articles from copper, brass, bronze and other alloys; some of which were unique to the country. Finely modelled figures and other pieces dating from the seventh and eighth centuries A.D. are known, and the great bronze figure, the Kamakura Daibutsu dates from 1252. The art of sword-mounting—the elaborate fashioning of the metal guard (*tsuba*), pommel (*kashira*), hilt-grips (*menuki*) and other parts—began seriously in the fifteenth century and continued until the wearing of the sword was abolished in 1876.

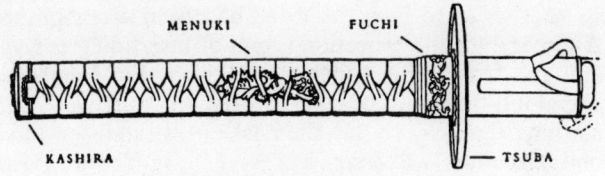

Figure 2. Handle of a Japanese sword.

The craftsmen making sword mounts were known as *sokenshi*, and as a branch of their work many of them made metal *ojime:* the bead on the cord by which objects were suspended from the girdle of a costume. Metal *ojime* are less rare than metal *netsuke*, and the latter mostly take the form of *kagamibuta*, and *kanabuta*; in which a mirror or a decorated metal plaque is set in a wood or ivory frame. Some of them date from the late eighteenth century, but mostly they are later. In the last quarter of the nineteenth century many makers of *kagamibuta* were working in Tokyo.

Amongst many other Japanese metal objects to be found

in Western collections may be listed: *Yatate*, portable writing-cases holding brushes and ink-slab; *Kana-dari*, washing-bowls; *Yuwakashi*, kettles; and *Kanemono*, mounts for tobacco-pouches and other objects. The great majority of these have a finish in their workmanship that betrays at once their country of origin, even when this is not revealed immediately by the style of ornament, and it is true to say that no nation has yet excelled the Japanese in metalwork.

The craftsmen were extremely skilful in the difficult art of inlaying and this was done not only in gold or silver, with and without niello, but a special form known as *sumi-zōgan*, Ink-inlaying, was perfected. The effect is that of a sketch drawn on the metal in Indian ink, and it was achieved by cutting out the design in one metal, hollowing out a shaped space in another to receive the first and then hammering the one into the other until they blended imperceptibly, and gave no clue as to how the work had been accomplished.

Another difficult decoration is that of Insertion (*kiribame*) where the front of a panel might show, for instance, a cockerel full-face, and the reverse reveal the back view of the same bird. To achieve this the cockerel is modelled in the round, and fitted into a space cut-out for it. The work calls for great skill and accuracy to ensure that no space whatsoever is visible on either surface when the figure is fitted in place and neatly soldered. In this and other equally complicated techniques the Japanese were highly proficient, and if much of their work fails to reach the highest standards it is because the buyers demanded no better and would not pay the price for the best.

Most of the wares will be found to be decorated with representations, usually realistic in character, of insects, flowers and leaves, birds, animals and, especially on cheaper pieces, views of Mount Fujiyama; the quiescent volcano rising to a height of over 12,000 ft. It has been described by travellers as the most beautiful in the world, and merits its name *Fujiyama*, or 'peerless mount'.

COPPER AND ITS ALLOYS

The *cire perdue* method of casting was employed exclusively, and the examples of finished work show that the makers were able to use the minimum of metal consistent with strength. Some of the colossal outdoor bronze figures (the Lochana Buddha at Nara is 138 ft. in height), were made most cleverly in sections; one section being cast at a time and joined to the preceding one. The sections are each about 12 ins. high, but the head and neck were made in a single piece measuring 12 ft.

The greatest skill was expended in the final finishing of a piece, the work of the metal-sculptor (*kinozoku-shi*). His chisels were divided methodically into thirty-six types, each with a name, and the types comprised up to ten varieties apiece, making a total in many instances of some 250 chisels and gravers.

Much first-class work was done in the later eighteenth century and during the first half of the nineteenth century. Among the eminent workers of those times may be included Seimin, Masatune, Teijo, Sōmin, Keisai, Takusai, and Gido. Later exponents, and their specialities include Murakami Takejoro (lanterns of copper and bronze), Kanazu Sorosaburo (kettles), Nagasaka Jujiro (flower vases and water pots), and the brothers Oshima Katsujiro and Oshima Yasutaro who traded under the name of Sanseisha.

The reading of signatures on Japanese pieces is made no easier by the fact that most artists and craftsmen adopted an 'art name' or pseudonym, also the Japanese characters can be written in two distinct forms (block-letter and script), but can be read in as many as two, sometimes four, different ways. Additionally, the art-name is sometimes found to have the word *sai* (studio) following, and any title with which the craftsman may have been honoured would form part of the signature.

Copper articles decorated with *cloisonné* enamel were made in Japan at about the same time as the process began to be used in China: sometime during the fifteenth century.

It was, however, employed less extensively than in the latter country until the early nineteenth century, when Kaji Tsunekichi established a studio for its manufacture in Nagoya. Later, further work of the same type was done at Yokohama and Tokyo. Most of the ware was destined for export with a marked emphasis on size and brilliant colour. In spite of this the workmanship was generally good, but the Japanese pieces made then and later are usually less attractive (at least to English eyes) than comparable Chinese ones. Some of the productions were simply direct copies of early Chinese pieces, but even when the tell-tale legend under the base, MADE IN JAPAN, has been removed, the colours and shape and the light weight are evidence that all is not well.

Russia. Articles of copper and brass were made in Russia, and some of them were decorated with enamel. Ikons, plaques modelled with representations of Christ, the Virgin Mary, or one or more saints, are found with coloured enamel ornament, but most are of recent date in spite of their appearance. Few are older than the nineteenth century, and it has been suggested that many of them were made solely for export to be sold to foreign collectors of the antique.

Of more artistic importance and much rarer are the articles decorated with copper and brass from the Imperial arms factory at Tula. This was founded in 1705 at a town about 120 miles south of Moscow, and although its principal role was to produce arms for the Russian army a certain amount of metalwork was manufactured from about 1765 for more peaceful purposes. Most of this was mainly of cut or blued steel, and a pair of candles in the Victoria and Albert Museum, London, is of this metal with typical additional ornament inlaid in gilt bronze. In appearance they give no hint that they are not of west European origin, and much of this Russian work is doubtless confused with French and English work of the late eighteenth century.

It may be mentioned that each of the candlesticks in question consists of twenty-seven separate parts assembled on a central spindle.

In the same museum is a fireplace, fender, and set of mantelshelf ornaments also of cut steel, with gilt brass and gilt copper decoration, made at Tula in the first years of the nineteenth century. In all probability this is the fireplace traced as having been mentioned in a letter of 1806, together with candlesticks and a 'Machine for perfuming the rooms'.

Later in the nineteenth century brass Samovars were made at Tula. These are the tea-urns, incorporating an internal heating device, that in Western minds are as synonymous with Russian life as vodka and the ballet.

Spain. Spanish craftsmen worked in both copper and its alloys. Comparatively little of their output is to be seen outside Spain itself, where some of the cathedrals and churches retain their fifteenth- and sixteenth-century bronze screens. From the same period date the bronze pulpits, of which there are fine examples at Burgos and Toledo.

Sweden. In the past, Sweden was noted more for the production of copper ore than for manufactured articles. A writer of 1735 noted that the ore was 'found in mines in several parts of Europe, but most abundantly in Sweden'. At Falun, in Dalecarlia in the west midlands of the country, are copper mines that were at one time among the largest in Europe.

Venice. The Venetian Republic was a highly important cultural centre in Europe for many centuries, and its traders were to be found in every civilized land. Those in Egypt acquired a liking for the locally-made inlaid brass wares, and eventually, in the late fifteenth century, a number of these metalworkers settled in Venice. They continued to make the types of articles to which they had long been accustomed, but working far from their home their designs often deviated from the traditional. Some of their work is quite indistinguishable from that done in their native land, but other pieces show clear traces of Italian and other European influences in both shape and decoration.

A late fifteenth-century ewer in the Victoria and Albert Museum, London, has both the handle and the spout in the form of dragons, a common feature on ewers from Germany and the Low Countries, and the inlaid and engraved decoration includes a coat-of-arms showing it was made for a member of an Italian family.

Eventually, the Venetians began to imitate the work of the foreign craftsmen and the latter returned to their own country or turned to other trades. Of the pieces made in Venice by members of this foreign colony, many are completely Islamic in appearance, others are of Italian form but with Eastern decoration, and the rarest are those of European shape but with Islamic ornamentation.

PART TWO

A Dictionary of Articles made from Copper and its Alloys

A Dictionary of Articles
made from
Copper and its Alloys

Ale and spirit measures. Standard measures were made in the eighteenth and nineteenth centuries in England so that an innkeeper could provide a legally correct amount of drink. Many of those made in London were of bronze, and they are in two shapes: straight-sided, and baluster or curved. When complete they are usually in sets of six, comprising the following: Quart, Pint, Half-pint, Gill, Half-gill and Drop. In some instances there is also a Half-gallon measure, but this is almost as rare as it is to find the Drop size in a normal set; being small, pocketable, and the most decorative and appealing, it is missing all too often.

Figure 3.

Measures of a large-bellied shape, the insides tinned heavily, and with small-sized flared mouths, were made of copper. They were in sets ranging from Five Gallons down to a Drop, and occasionally an even larger one is found. While the small sizes were for use in serving spirits in public houses, the larger were employed in distilleries for measuring accurately the amount put into a barrel. Alternatively, they were for diluting full-strength gin and rum so that it might be less harmful to the drinker. Earlier versions of them were made of a thicker gauge of metal than the more modern ones, and although both types resemble an enlarged onion in outline the older ones are more bulbous at the base. Again, the Drop size is a rarity, but more so with these measures than with others. Due to the lack of this smallest measure there are far more incomplete sets of all kinds than there are complete ones.

Ale warmers. Mulled ale is made with warm ale, sugar, spices and other ingredients. To heat the drink it was put into a copper ale warmer: a container shaped like a slipper or shoe, of which the 'toe' was put among the glowing embers of the fire. Surviving specimens are rarely older than the nineteenth century, and are often mistaken for boot-warmers. Another type was made to hang on the bars of a grate, and has a spout from which the beverage can be poured. A third variety is conical in shape, and was used mostly in the western counties of England where it is known as a 'donkey's ear'. The pointed base is set in the fire, and it has an iron handle with which to hold it when pouring.

Alms dishes. Dishes both shallow and deep and varying in diameter from about nine inches to some two feet, are assumed to have been made for the collecting of alms. They are of sheet brass hammered with designs in relief, and with the outer rim rolled neatly to give strength. Most are embossed with Biblical scenes, and with a band of Gothic lettering. This latter is often merely decorative; the makers having taken letters of the alphabet at random and used them for filling a border without any regard to their forming intelligible words. The dishes were made principally in the south of Germany from the later years of the fifteenth century, and must have been produced in considerable numbers judging by the fact that survivors are not particularly scarce.

Andirons and fire-dogs. In the earliest mansions the fireplace was in the centre of the great hall, the smoke rising

A DICTIONARY OF COPPER ARTICLES

and finding an exit through a hole left for it in the roof. Improvement came when the hearth was sited in a side wall of the room and a shaft was built to carry away the smoke. At this stage, the chimney-piece, framing the opening where the fire burned, began to be decorated in a manner that emphasized its importance, and at the same time, the apparatus for fire-making received attention.

Andirons are metal bearers on which logs can rest while they burn. Each takes the form of an upright resting on two feet, with a horizontal bar fixed low down at right angles and bent downwards at the far end to form a third foot. The horizontal member, known as the billet bar, supports the blazing wood and is almost always of iron, but the uprights, while also usually of the same metal, are often overlaid with brass, bronze, or even silver.

Italian examples, dating from the sixteenth and seventeenth centuries, have designs either cast or engraved on them, and are topped by vase-shaped finials. Others, from the same country, are in the form of mythological figures in bronze, and were the work of artists of the first rank. A pair, with bronze figures representing Apollo and Mercury, standing 35 in. high, fetched no less than 9,200 guineas (about $27,000) at the dispersal of the collection formed by John Edward Taylor, sold by auction in London in 1912.

Another type of andiron was decorated in the so-called Surrey enamel, with the uprights faced with plates of brass. These were cast with a pattern of shallow depressions filled with coloured enamels to form a pattern. A pair of this description is known that bear the Royal Arms of the Stuarts, and date from about 1670.

Fire-dogs are similar in both appearance and use to andirons, but are smaller in size. In the seventeenth century in England a pair of each would stand in the same fireplace, the logs resting on the fire-dogs which were usually less highly decorated. When coal replaced wood as the everyday fuel, and a raised grate became general for burning it, the andiron and fire-dog ceased to be made for their original purpose. They became of no practical importance and were used only as decoration, or as a support for fire-irons.

Eighteenth-century French fire-dogs (in French called *chenets*) are usually made of ormolu, and their design reflects the prevailing style of the period in which they were manufactured. Examples of the Louis XV and Louis XVI periods were reproduced throughout the nineteenth century, and genuine examples are rare.

In America the famous silversmith, Paul Revere of Boston (1735–1818), turned his attention to making articles of brass and copper, and a pair of brass andirons bearing his mark are in the Metropolitan Museum of Art, New York. They have front legs of cabriole shape with ball-and-claw feet supporting tall uprights with square bases and bulbous columns, and finials ornamented with 'wrythen' reeding.

Aquamaniles. An aquamanile, the word means literally 'hand washer', is a bronze or brass jug, usually with a cover, for holding water at the table. They were in use from the twelfth to the fifteenth centuries before forks were commonly employed, and when the fingers of a diner got sticky and greasy during meals. Water was poured over the hands from the aquamanile into a basin between courses.

It was made either in the form of a human figure or of an animal; in the case of the latter, usually with the tail curled over the back to form a handle. The lion was a very popular model, although the connexion between the king of the jungle and hand-washing is far from clear. Some of the human-type aquamaniles were fitted with a plain handle at the back, but others incorporated an animal or some fanciful feature that was adapted adroitly by the modeller into a handle.

Aquamaniles were made both on the Continent and in England, and it is not easy to determine on which side of the Channel many of them originated. Great interest centred on these objects some fifty or so years ago, and they were then given attention by fakers. Medieval examples were made by the *cire perdue* method, whereas the forgeries came from moulds and traces of mould-marks will be visible; even the cleverest counterfeiter usually fails to hide all his tracks. Genuine examples are very rarely on the market, and most of them are to be found now in museums.

Bedsteads. The brass bedstead was not so long ago the butt of music-hall jokes, but having attained its centenary must now be considered almost as an antique. Once a commonplace, it is now becoming a rare sight and probably few of the present growing generation can remember seeing one in use.

The metal bedstead replaced that of wood soon after Queen Victoria came to the throne, and was helped to public favour by its hygienic qualities. In spite of this, although metal was obviously cleaner, the designers imitated carved woodwork as nearly as they could and made the new bedsteads complete with innumerable interstices for harbouring dust and germs. The earlier examples of brass bedsteads were well represented in the 1851 Exhibition. The public then saw, among others, a large four-post bedstead cast with figures and scrollwork and hung with green silk curtains, advertised by the maker as being in the Renaissance style. The same manufacturer showed two brass cots for babies; both suspended from scrolled arms, and one surmounted at the head by the figure of a winged angel to support a muslin canopy.

Brass bedsteads of less complicated pattern, consisting of tubes joined together and topped by spheres of different sizes, did not become current until towards the end of the nineteenth century. By that time also, the corner posts and curtains had been dispensed with, and the bedstead had a head and a foot; the latter often nearly as tall as the head. These bedsteads were not of solid brass, but of thin sheets of the metal on a core of cast-iron. The usual finish was that of giving the surface a high polish and then covering it with lacquer. Cheaper versions were made of black japanned cast-iron with a minimum of brass ornament to relieve the gloom.

Bells. The bell appears to be one of the most simple metal devices, but this simplicity belies the thought that has been put into it over the centuries. Special alloys and special techniques of casting have been developed, and a great amount of study devoted both to founding and to the art of bell-ringing.

Bell-metal varies in the proportion of its principal ingredients: copper and tin. The result has to be strong and hard, and it has an unfortunate tendency to crack if the actual casting is faulty, or if the ringer is unskilled or careless. The casting itself was performed at a number of centres, but in the past was also the work of itinerant men such as Miles Graye who flourished in East Anglia during the mid-seventeenth century. He, and others of his trade, did the casting on the spot, probably re-melting broken or unwanted bells to provide the new. They dug pits for the foundry fire and for the casting moulds, and when their work was done they went on to the next village where their services were needed.

Although the shape and proportions of a bell are now, more or less, standardized, this was not always the case and it is sometimes possible to identify the age and country of origin of a specimen from its form. In Europe, the familiar trumpet-mouthed shape was in general use by about the sixteenth century, but was preceded by many variants including some that were long and narrow, mitre-shaped, and quadrangular. Some authorities give the diameter of a bell as ten times the thickness of its edge and the thickness multiplied by twelve to give the height, but these figures are no more than a rough guide. Each maker had his personal variations.

It is thought that bells were seldom used in Europe before the sixth century A.D., and in England, Bede, the historian, wrote of one at Whitby Abbey, in Yorkshire, in the year 680. Surviving bells of such an early date are few in number, small in size and made from iron plates riveted together. It was not until later that alloys of copper were used and developed for the purpose, and by the fifteenth century specimens of up to 25,000 pounds in weight were cast with success. It may be mentioned that the earliest English bell of undisputable age is one dated 1296 in Lancashire, but undated specimens may be older.

Bronze portable bells, with a handle by which they can be shaken, were made in Italy and elsewhere from the fifteenth century. Some were the work of eminent artists, and much thought was given to their design and execution. Needless to say, they are very rare and innumerable copies of later date exist. The hand-bell was used for the purpose of summoning servants and to announce the readiness of a meal; in the latter case, to quote the words of the late Percy Scholes, 'by some considered of all instruments to supply the sweetest music'.

A simple form of bell was made from a small sheet of bronze bent nearly double, and with the sides riveted. With a clapper inside and a plain handle at the top, this was used to hang round the necks of animals. The owners of sheep, cows, goats, etc., could then hear where they had strayed and recover them in due course. They appear to have been in use throughout Europe, and occasionally examples are found with incised or punched ornament, but most are quite plain.

Braziers. A brazier is, in effect, a portable fireplace, and it stands in a room without a hearth, in one with an inadequate hearth, or in one where heating is wanted only temporarily. It has been in use for a long time, and a thirteenth-century Syrian specimen is in the Metropolitan Museum, New York. This is of brass inlaid elaborately with silver and inscribed with the name of the Sultan al-Malik al-Muzaffar Yusuf, a ruler of the Yemen. Two Sultans bore this name, but it is assumed that the brazier was made for the earlier who was in power from 1249 until 1295.

Although very popular in the East, the brazier was not unknown in the West. In England, it is recorded at least as early as the sixteenth century, and references in documents of the time of Henry VIII to grates mounted on wheels refer most probably to braziers. Specimens made in the early eighteenth century have survived, and these take the form of tall iron stands of plain design each fitted at the top with a copper bowl. The bowls have pierced lids, the holes allowing air to reach the glowing charcoal within.

They were made also in other European countries, including Spain. There, a decorative low-standing circular type, with an elaborately pierced and domed lid, was made of brass in the eighteenth century.

Buckets and Cauldrons. Bronze buckets and cauldrons dating from the Late Bronze Age have been excavated, or found in the beds of rivers. One of the former, with a capacity in the region of two gallons, from a cave in Co. Durham, is in the British Museum. Also on exhibition there is a cauldron, found in the River Thames near Battersea, built up from plates of metal riveted together and with two handles at opposite sides of the upper rim. Later types have one long swinging handle so that the vessel can be suspended over an open fire, and the contents tipped out at either side when needed. The open cauldron was referred to often in the past as a Kettle, and this term is still used for it in America.

Large-sized bronze buckets do not seem to have been common, but possibly those that were made had heavy usage which may account for the lack of surviving examples. Cast bronze cauldrons superseded the riveted type, and they remained popular until replaced in course of time by those made of iron.

Small containers for holy water used in the church were made of bronze. Some of them are in the form of miniature buckets; the swinging handles making it convenient for them to be carried during a service. Most of these articles for ecclesiastical purposes were usually heavily decorated with cast and chiselled patterns, and in most cases these are, appropriately, of Biblical subjects. In contrast, the larger buckets and cauldrons for domestic use were severely practical in design and almost free of ornamentation; the most they have is a band or two of engraved or stamped pattern of a conventional type.

Eighteenth-century buckets of mahogany, bound with hoops of brass in the manner of barrels, were popular for a number of purposes. Those with a vertical slit an inch or more in width were for carrying plates to and from kitchen and dining-room; others were for holding logs or peat. Oval-shaped tubs of similar pattern were made for displaying plants, or to hold ice for cooling wine. Of the latter, some were made octagonal in shape with a hinged lid, and raised on short legs to a convenient height. The name of 'Torbat, celleret-maker, 36 Red Lion Street, London', recorded in the late eighteenth century, almost certainly refers to a maker who specialized in these particular articles, but it has not been possible yet to identify his actual work.

Dutch mahogany buckets of double-elliptical shape with bowed upper edges, known as *Teestoofs*, date from the same period and also later. These are brass-bound, and fitted originally with a brass lining were used for holding charcoal to keep tea-kettles hot.

Buttons. The use and wearing of buttons goes back far in history, but specimens of a date earlier than the eighteenth century are rarely found. The interest of collectors is limited perforce to that century and later, when they became increasingly fashionable and were made in great quantity.

The manufacture of buttons was an important trade in England from the eighteenth century, so much so that Parliament made the importation of foreign ones illegal.

Further, fabric-covered buttons might not be worn at all without the risk of incurring severe penalties, and this greatly assisted the growing metal trades.

Birmingham was the headquarters of the manufacture of metal buttons, which were made there first in about 1660. Matthew Boulton of the Soho Works was one of the largest makers a century later, and introduced a number of improved processes. In button-making he was no less successful than in the other branches of his extensive business.

James Watt, the Scottish inventor of the steam engine, wrote a *Memoir* of Boulton and recorded in it his first acquaintance with the factory of his future business partner:

'I was introduced at Soho by Dr Small in 1767, but Mr Boulton was then absent; Mr Fothergill, his partner, and Dr Small showed me the works. The goods then manufactured were steel, gilt, and fancy buttons, steel watch chains and sword hilts, plated wares, ornamental works in ormolu, tortoiseshell snuff boxes, Bath metal buttons inlaid with steel, and various other articles which I have now forgot. A mill with a water wheel was employed in laminating metal for the buttons, plated goods, etc., and to turn laps for grinding and polishing steel work, and I was informed that Mr Boulton was the first inventor of the inlaid buttons, and the first who had applied a mill to turn the laps. Besides the lap in the mill, I saw . . . a shaking box put in motion by the mill for scouring button blanks and other small pieces of metal; which was also a thought of Mr B.'

Dr Samuel Johnson visited Soho in 1774, and was struck by the fact that Boulton could sell a gross of buttons for as little as 12*s*. It should be mentioned, however, that at about that same date the wholesale price varied between 3*d* and £7 a gross according to material and finish.

Button-making was described in detail by a writer in 1764, as follows:

'*The manner of making Metal Buttons.* The metal with which the moulds are intended to be covered is first cast into small ingots, and then flattened into thin plates or leaves, of the thickness intended, at the flatting-mills; after which it is cut into small round pieces proportionable to the size of the mould they are intended to cover, by means of proper punches on a block of wood covered with a thick plate of lead. Each piece of metal thus cut out of the plate is reduced into the form of a button, by beating it successively in several cavities, or concave moulds, of a spherical form, with a convex puncheon of iron, always beginning with the shallowest cavity or mould, and proceeding to the deeper, till the plate has acquired the intended form: and the better to manage so thin a plate, they form ten, twelve and sometimes even twenty-four to the cavities, or concave moulds, at once, often annealing the metal during the operation, to make it more ductile. This plate is generally called by workmen, the cap of the button.

'The form being thus given to the plates, or caps, they strike the intended impression on the convex side by means of a similar iron puncheon in a kind of mould engraven en creux (cut in), either by the hammer, or the press used in coining. The cavity of the mould, wherein the impression is to be made, is of a diameter and depth suitable to the sort of button intended to be struck in it; each kind requiring a particular mould. Between the puncheon and the plate is placed a thin piece of lead, called by workmen a hob, which greatly contributes to the taking off all the strokes of the engraving; the lead by reason of its softness, easily giving way to the parts that have relievo (are in relief); and as easily insinuating itself into the traces or indentures.

'The plate thus prepared makes the cap or shell of the button. The lower part is formed of another plate, in the same manner, but much flatter, and without any impression. To the last or under plate is soldered a small eye made of wire, by which the button is to be fastened.

'The two plates being thus finished, they are soldered together with soft solder, and then turned in a lathe. Generally indeed they use a wooden mould instead of the under plate; and in order to fasten it, they pass a thread or gut across through the middle of the mould, and fill the cavity between the mould and the cap with cement in order to render the button firm and solid; for the cement entering all the cavities formed by the relievo of the other side sustains it, prevents it flattening, and preserved its bosse or design.'

Later improvements included William Bell's patent of 1779 for impressing designs 'by means of rolling cylinders on which such dies are engraved'. This meant that impressions could be taken at speed by means of a rotary press rather like an old-fashioned clothes wringer.

Buttons were made also in a single piece with the eye cast in one with the button, and after being polished these were gilded. In a letter of the time the writer specified the following for his newly ordered clothing: 'The buttons to be metal buttons with eyes of the same, not buttons with wooden molds and catgut loops which are good for nothing. They must be gilt with gold, and wrought in imitation of buttons made with thread or wire.' In other words, they should be made of brass throughout, either composed of parts and dome-shaped or else cast in one piece, and resemble in appearance buttons covered in gold wire. This latter effect could be obtained in three ways: by stamping the hollow article, by casting the design when making the solid, or even by engraving on the flat casting.

In other civilized countries of the world the wearing of

buttons was just as fashionable, and therefore essential, as it was in England. Each had its own different processes, but the finished products were generally similar in appearance to each other and it is often difficult now to tell them apart.

America imported the greater proportion of her needs until the nineteenth century, and then her own industry was soon sufficiently large to meet home demands. However, as early as 1750 there were attempts to supply the native market, and Caspar Wistar of Philadelphia tried his hand at button-making before he removed to New Jersey and turned to a more lucrative trade in which he achieved fame: glass-making. An advertisement in a New York newspaper of September, 1750, reads as follows:

> 'Whereas I Henry Witeman having served my Apprenticeship with Caspar Wister, Brass Button-Maker in Philadelphia, have now set up the same Business in New-York, where all Persons that shall please to favour me with their Custom, may depend on having the work done in the best Manner, and at reasonable Rates; at my Shop in Maiden-Lane, between the Fly-Market and the New Dutch Church.'

Ten years later Witeman (or Whiteman) advertised that 'As there are a great many of the counterfeit Sort sold in this City for Philadelphia Buttons, which, upon Trial, have been found to break very soon, and the Purchasers thereof considerably imposed upon; he gives this Notice to the Publick, that he calls those of his Make, New-York Buttons, which has been well tried amongst all his Customers, and from whom he had heard no Complaint.' By that date, he had removed to an address 'At the Sign of the Buttons and Buckles, near the Oswego Market'.

By the end of the century activity had increased, and in 1793, Messrs Cornwell and Martin, from Birmingham, 'respectfully inform their friends and the public in general, they have established a manufactory for gilt and plated buttons, at Corlear's Hook, New York'. In the following year, Shotwell and James, of 214 Pearl Street, N.Y., require the services of 'a person well acquainted with the manufactory of Mathewman's Hard Metal Buttons'; which sounds suspiciously like an attempt at 'poaching'.

The dome-shaped buttons, of which the making has been described above, and the one-piece cast type were both fashionable throughout most of the eighteenth and nineteenth centuries, but variations in style came and went with the years. Whereas a Georgian gentleman might have brass or gilt buttons on his outdoor coats, he usually had plated ones on his best indoor clothing and the wealthier sported silver, gold or faceted polished steel. A vogue for the wearing of oversize buttons was noticeable between 1775 and 1790, and it is said that the maximum in England was reached in 1777. Towards the end of the eighteenth century, both in France and England there was a large output of buttons enamelled with coloured designs on copper.

Button-collecting is a hobby that has many adherents all over the world. In the United States of America enthusiasts have formed a National Button Society, which has its own publication for recording information on the subject.

Candlesticks and candelabra. Undoubtedly the introduction of the candle involved also the making of the first candlestick. When these two events may have taken place is a matter for conjecture, but probably the first candle-holders were of clay, either sun-dried or baked in a fire. The earliest surviving metal candlesticks would appear to date from the eleventh and twelfth centuries.

The most celebrated of them is the Gloucester Candlestick, at one time in the Benedictine Monastery of St Peter, Gloucester, and in the thirteenth century presented to the French cathedral at Le Mans. In the mid-nineteenth century it was in the possession of a family living in the town of Le Mans, and after changing hands yet again has been in the

Victoria and Albert Museum, London, since 1861. The Gloucester Candlestick is made of gilt bell-metal, and was cast by the *cire perdue* process in an astonishingly complicated pattern of what has been described aptly as a 'fantastic ballet of men, monkeys and monsters'. There is little doubt that it was made for use at the Altar, and that at one time it formed a pair with another which is now lost.

There are several survivors of early examples of another type of Church light: the Paschal candlestick or candelabra in which an enormous candle burned continuously for the six weeks between Easter and Whitsun. One of the most splendid was once in Durham Cathedral: it was almost as wide as the Choir and the principal light correspondingly tall, and with the great central candle in its place the whole towered nearly 70 ft. high into the vaulted roof. Known as 'one of the rarest monuments in all England', this did not prevent its partial destruction at the time of the Reformation. Although the arms were then removed, the base was soon mounted with a figure of an eagle to become a lectern until it, too, was finally discarded. Surviving Paschal candlesticks of great age may be seen still in a few churches on the Continent: in Italy, Germany and Belgium. The 14 ft. high gilt bronze one in Milan Cathedral is especially noteworthy in spite of the fact that is has been there only since 1562, and its earlier history remains unknown.

The origin of this and other Paschal candlesticks has been disputed from time to time, as there is little evidence by which to prove any one nation to have been responsible for their making. Many of the elements of their design were common to more than one people, and it seems probable that they will continue to be debated in the future.

Also of religious significance is the Jewish Hanukkah lamp: a candelabra for eight lights, either for candles, oil, or both, and made in the form of a low rectangular tray or as a tall eight-armed lamp-stand. In both instances the lights, whether oil or candle, are arranged in a line. It is used in both homes and synagogues during the feast of Dedication or Hanukkah, and celebrates the miracle of the single flask of oil remaining in the Temple after it had been defiled by Antiochus Epiphanes, king of Syria. The oil, sufficient normally for a single day's use, continued to give light for eight days; the legend is recorded in 2 Maccabees, i, 18, one of the Apocryphal books of the Old Testament. While most brass and copper examples of these lamps are of modern manufacture, there are a number of surviving examples of eighteenth-century date made in various countries in Europe. There are several from Poland in the Victoria and Albert Museum, London.

Turning to candlesticks for secular use it will be found that there are very few early examples to be seen; which is not remarkable considering the hard wear they must have suffered from continual use. One, of Saracenic brass is in the Victoria and Albert Museum, and is ornamented typically with an elaborate pattern inlaid in silver and black pigment. Among the decoration are panels showing animals, birds and the fabulous Waqwaq tree: a tree that was supposed to be able to talk in every language, and whose branches end in bird and animal heads. The candlestick has a short stem beneath the candle-holder, and the tall spreading drum-shaped base gives it a total height of 14 in. The base of a similar candlestick, perhaps made for the Sultan Badr-ad-Din Lulu of Mosul, who died in the year 1259, is in the Metropolitan Museum, New York.

From the thirteenth century onwards candlesticks of bronze formed a proportion of the prolific output of the many founders in the area of Dinant on the River Meuse. These latter holders often took unexpected forms: for instance, the base would be in the shape of a grotesque animal and the greasepan, to catch drips from the candle, an opened flower; or, as a lion with Samson on his back and the candle-socket growing uncomfortably from the middle of the latter's neck. Many Continental examples were fitted with a spike, or *Pricket*, to hold the candle, but this slowly went out of general use and the familiar socket replaced it almost everywhere.

The circular base rising to a stem appears on many early seventeenth-century candlesticks, and about half-way up the shaft is a round drip-catcher or greasepan. Often this is of the same diameter as the base, and it is usually slightly dished to retain the spilled wax. By the middle years of the century brass candlesticks were being made in quantity, although survivors are now becoming uncommon. Their pattern was more or less standardized, and it is a matter of argument in many instances as to where particular specimens were made. Those with simply turned columns and trumpet-shaped bases are ascribed usually to England, and others with moulded bases and elaborately turned shafts to the Continent.

It is said that English brass candlesticks rarely, if ever, have a hole at the side of the candle-socket by which a spike of some kind could be inserted to remove the burned-down stump. Candlesticks found in England with this feature, and they are not uncommon, probably are of Flemish or Dutch origin.

Early in the eighteenth century the large greasepan was replaced by a much smaller one at the very top of the socket instead of in the middle of the shaft. In due course, this was moulded in one piece with a collar which was removable from the socket, and is sometimes missing from surviving specimens. A sliding device with a protruding thumbpiece was fitted occasionally in the shafts of candlesticks of this date and later, and by moving the slider the candle could be raised and lowered or ejected. The base often assumed a square shape, and while some were octagonal or hexagonal, others had the corners curved or canted (cut off), and a further type was scalloped. By about 1760 the base had become completely square and rose to a straight shaft, but later there was a fashion for oval bases. In Italy a triangular base for pricket candlesticks of all sizes was very popular, but it cannot be said that this was exclusively a feature of candlesticks from that source. The many styles overlap one another in date and each was imitated quickly by makers in other countries.

Most of the seventeenth- and eighteenth-century designs for brass candlesticks have remained popular since their first introduction, and have been reproduced almost continuously ever since. Early seventeenth-century examples were usually cast in two parts: stem and base, either screwing together or with a projecting tongue from the stem that was then burred over inside the base. Later candlesticks were hollow, and some were made with a central iron rod to hold the parts together.

Gilt bronze, or ormolu, was used by the French and other nations towards the end of the seventeenth century. The designs reached their heights of extravagance in about 1740, when the rococo style was at its greatest popularity. It is as well to remember that many of the typical Louis XIV, XV and XVI patterns were reproduced continuously throughout the nineteenth century—and later. They were copied and adapted about 1760 in England, where Matthew Boulton and probably other metalworkers made ormolu of high quality that is confused easily with French work.

A good idea of the extent of use to which the candle was put, shortly before the alternative of the much brighter Argand oil-lamp was invented, is provided by a German visitor to London. Georg Lichtenberg wrote of a walk he took down Cheapside at eight o'clock on a winter's evening in 1775, and described the scene as follows:

> 'On both sides tall houses with plate-glass windows. The lower floors consist of shops and seem to be made entirely of plate glass; many thousand candles light up silverware, engravings, books, clocks, pewter, paintings, women's finery, modish and otherwise, gold, precious stones,

steel-work and endless coffee-rooms and lottery offices. The street looks as though it were illuminated for some festivity: the apothecaries and druggists display glasses filled with gay-coloured spirits ... which ... suffuse many a wide space with a purple, yellow, verdigris-green, or azure light.'

In England in the early nineteenth century there was a fashion for bronze, or bronze and ormolu, candlesticks, some of them hung with cut-glass prisms. They vary greatly in quality, and some of the less expensive ones were decorated with ornament stamped on thin sheets of bronze or brass, dark brown or gilt in colour.

The Victorian period saw the introduction of little that was new; it was a period when the oil lamp rapidly replaced the candle. The sole innovation would seem to be the folding candle-holder: there were a number of types of these made for the use of railway travellers. They incorporate a hook for affixing to the lapel of a coat or jacket or to a seat-back, and it is perhaps remarkable that there were not innumerable cases of fire arising from their use.

The *chamber* or *bedroom candlestick* usually has a comparatively large tray, either round or oblong in shape, and a curled handle often with a thumbpiece conveniently on the top. Many were made of brass both in England and on the Continent, the latter favouring a pattern with a long handle giving the article a resemblance to a frying pan. Most of them were made complete with a cone-shaped extinguisher.

CANDELABRA. A holder for more than one candle no doubt was made very soon after that for a single light. Apart from those in the churches they would not seem to have been very popular, and the earliest brass ones are no older than the seventeenth century. As with candlesticks of the time, it is not easy to distinguish where they were made, but probably they were introduced in Flanders and copied in England.

Few were made in the eighteenth century, candelabra then were mostly of silver and, later, of Sheffield plate.

In France, from the late seventeenth century onwards, very fine pairs of candelabra were made of ormolu, and some of those in the rococo Louis XV manner were copied in other countries. Not only were they made entirely of metal, but vases of porcelain, marble and other materials were mounted in ormolu and fitted with two or more holders for candles.

A form of candelabra is the so-called Student's Lamp, a utilitarian version of an earlier French ormolu two or three light candelabra. The Student's Lamp has two or three candle holders, with either one large shade or several individual ones, adjustable for height on a central column. They are found in both painted iron and in brass, and their simple design may explain why they are now named after the ever-impecunious scholar. Most probably they were used in offices in the nineteenth century, but now that most of them have been wired for electricity they can take their place in more sophisticated surroundings.

Censers. Censers for burning incense in church were made of bronze and specimens of early date have survived. Some have removable covers, pierced to let the smoke escape, others are open at the top. Most were made with chains by which they were held and swung from side to side, but another type has a handle at one side.

Cauldrons. *See* **Buckets.**

Chandeliers. The word chandelier is known to have been used in the fifteenth century, but did not come into general use to describe a hanging many-armed lighting appliance until during the first half of the eighteenth century. Before that, the words 'lustre', 'branch', 'hanging candlestick', and 'sconce' were employed indiscriminately to describe the same article. This confusion lasted until about 1770, and old written records are frequently the subject of argument by scholars when trying to decide just what is meant by one of these ambiguous terms.

Some of the early Christian churches were lit on occasion by a form of chandelier known as a *polycandelon*. This was a flat circular plate pierced with a number of holes to contain small glass vessels, each containing oil and a wick. A number of them would hang by chains from the roof of a church, and doubtless their weak and odorous light went some way towards relieving the gloom.

Following the polycandelon came the *corona*, which consisted of a hoop of metal on which were spikes to hold candles. One of these, at Hildesheim in Germany, dates from the eleventh century and has holders for seventy-two candles. It is made of gilded and enamelled copper with silver ornament, and at one time had round the circumference a number of figures of Old Testament characters and the twelve Apostles, but these were stolen in the seventeenth century. Other coronas of even larger size have been recorded but most of the early ones have been destroyed.

A fifteenth-century English document mentions a decorative and luxurious chandelier then in Durham Cathedral. In that great building, before the High Altar, 'were three marveilous faire silver Basins hung in chains of silver . . . thiese three silver basins had lattin (brass) basins within them having prickets for serges, or great wax candles, to stand on, the lattin basins beinge to receive the drops of the candles, which did burne continually both day and night, in token that the House was always watchinge to God'. These lights, with much else, have since disappeared.

At about this date brass chandeliers with arms were being made on the Continent, and many of them were of elaborate design. The curved arms were modelled with pierced ornament, and the central stem often had one or more figures; the latter usually of the Virgin or a saint. In most cases, the chandelier of the time was made principally of wood, with metal spikes and greasepans to hold the candles and catch drips. They were very much in the nature of luxuries, and their use was confined almost solely to important occasions.

Candles were expensive and their wicks had to have frequent attention, they gave out much heat and little light and it was not uncommon for drips of hot grease to ruin clothing or furnishings.

The fact that Henry IV and Richard III both made Orders forbidding the importation of 'hanging candlesticks' is interpreted as a protection for those being made in England. It is assumed that some types of brass chandeliers were then being manufactured; and in sufficient numbers to merit the stopping of supplies from other countries.

The seventeenth century saw the introduction of a pattern of brass chandelier that is still familiar and remains in current production after some three hundred years of popularity. The elegant many-armed brass chandelier was made first in Holland, and set a fashion imitated in many other countries. Examples of them hold from half a dozen candles up to as many as thirty or forty, the gracefully curved arms set in tiers springing from a central turned column, and the large polished globes of brass reflecting the light and giving the whole appliance a look of safety and solidity. Most examples have the central stem in parts held together by a strong iron rod, with the candle-arms hooking into spaces provided for them.

The Dutch brass chandelier was copied in England with success, and many examples remain intact in the churches in which they were first placed. Both London and the provinces had makers, and some of the extant chandeliers are engraved with the names of the men who made them. Almost every maker had his personal preference in shaping the arms, in the design of the finial or other features, and a close study enables examples sometimes to be attributed to a maker or a district on the ground of style.

The brass chandelier in England was employed almost exclusively in churches or in public buildings, whereas in Holland the same applied with the important addition that they were to be found also in the homes of the Dutch.

PLATE 1 (*Above*) Dutch engraved brass tobacco box, 18th century, 4¼ inches wide. PLATE 2 (*Below*) Indian bronze and gilt-bronze figures of deities, 2¼, 4½ and 1¼ inches high.

PLATE 3 (*Above left*) Italian bronze warrier on horseback, by Riccio, about 1500, 13½ inches high. PLATE 4 (*Above right* (Flemish (Dinant) bronze aquamanile, 15th century, 9¾ inches high. PLATE 5 (*Below*) English box lock engraved with the arms of William and Mary, about 1700, 8¾ inches long.

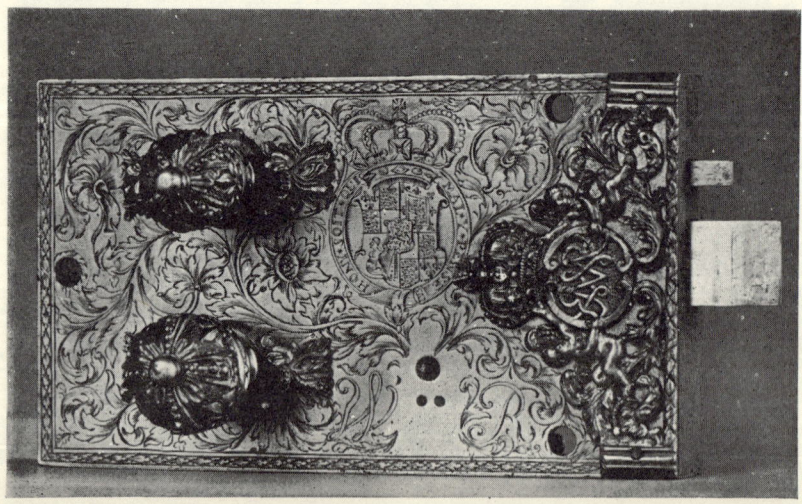

PLATE 6 (*above left*) Saracenic brass bucket with silver inlay, early 16th century. PLATE 7 (*Above right*) Indian vase of Bidri ware, 7½ inches high. PLATE 8 (*Below*) English copper tea-kettle with stand and lamp, 18th century, 13½ inches high.

PLATE 9 English brass furniture handles ranging from about 1660 (*top*) to about 1830 (*bottom*).

PLATE 10 English copper batterie-de-cuisine once owned by the first Duke of Wellington and now exhibited at the Royal Pavilion, Brighton.

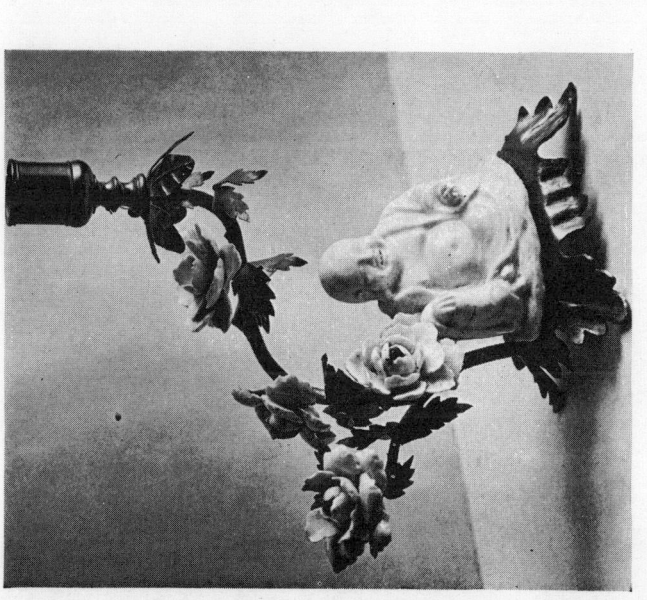

PLATE 11 (*Above*) French porcelain figure mounted in painted metal with porcelain flowers, 18th century, 9 inches high.
PLATE 12 (*Top right*) English bronze mortar moulded with the crowned head of Charles II, about 1680, 6¼ inches diameter.
PLATE 13 (*Right*) Tibetan bronze sacrificial cup, 18th century 5½ inches long.

PLATE 14 (*Above left*) Italian brass candlestick, 17th century, 18 inches high. PLATE 15 (*Above right*) South Indian copper statuette of the goddess Tara, 17th century, 7¾ inches high. PLATE 16 (*Below*) English (*two on left*) and Flemish (*two on right*) brass candlesticks, 17th century, tallest 11 inches high.

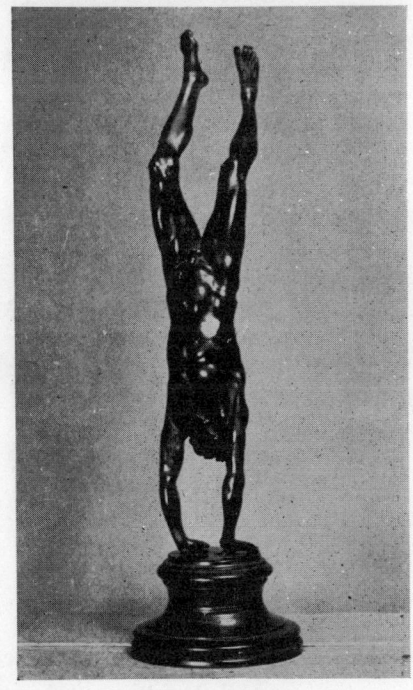

PLATE 17 (*Top*) English pierced and engraved brass fender, about 1730. PLATE 18 (*Above left*) French bronze and ormolu candelabrum, late 18th century, 28½ inches high. PLATE 19 (*Above right*) Italian bronze statuette of an acrobat, perhaps by Domenico Poggini, about 1550, 11½ inches high. PLATE 20 (*Left*) German brass alms dish, 17th century, 15¾ inches diameter.

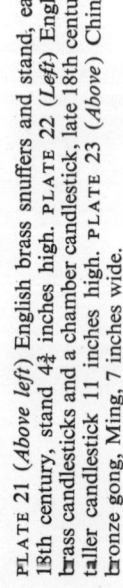
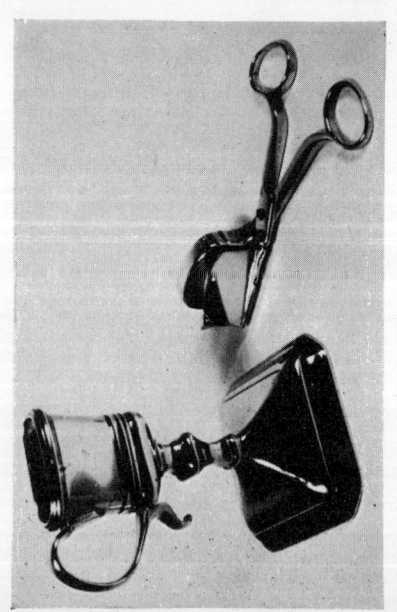

PLATE 21 (*Above left*) English brass snuffers and stand, early 18th century, stand 4¾ inches high. PLATE 22 (*Left*) English brass candlesticks and a chamber candlestick, late 18th century, taller candlestick 11 inches high. PLATE 23 (*Above*) Chinese bronze gong, Ming, 7 inches wide.

Paintings depicting house-interiors of the seventeenth and eighteenth centuries confirm that this was the case.

In the wealthier English homes of the seventeenth century there were chandeliers of solid silver, and others with metal (silver or brass) frames hung with faceted drops of rock crystal. These latter were introduced from France where, in 1649 when he was presented to Louis XIV, John Evelyn the diarist noted 'In the Presence [Chamber] hung 3 huge branches of Chrystal'. No doubt such foreign innovations were soon copied in England, but at this distance of time it is only rarely possible to say whether surviving chandeliers of these types in England were made there or on the Continent.

By the opening years of the eighteenth century the French metalworkers were making chandeliers of ormolu to conform in pattern with the prevailing taste. These early gilt chandeliers are of severe pattern when compared with later examples, and frequently used female heads as a part of their ornament. Some of them have been attributed to the workshop of the famous cabinet-maker, André-Charles Boulle; who is better known for his furniture veneered with brass and tortoiseshell.

With the coming to the throne of Louis XV the rococo style spread from France throughout Europe, and every form of art was affected by it. The French ormolu chandelier was no exception, and the swirling asymetrical lines of those from the hand of Jacques Caffieri, and his son Philippe, are among the most characteristic productions of the time. Two of them, both stamped with the name of Caffieri, and one dated 1751, are among the more important possessions of the Wallace Collection, London.

Not until about the beginning of the succeeding century did brass again play a part in the design of the English chandelier. Then, there came a fashion for chandeliers with a central hoop from which were suspended strings of glass drops gathered together at the base to form a bag. In some instances the hoop was of patterned gilt metal, and the candle-holders inside the cut-glass cups were of the same metal. Others, too, were fitted with gilt metal arms which radiated from the hoop.

Of the cost and complex design of some chandeliers of the period there is no lack of evidence. In the decoration of his favourite Royal Pavilion at Brighton the Prince Regent, later King George IV, spared no expense, and in the matter of light fittings he was as extravagant as in other directions. The Banqueting Room was furnished with a very large central chandelier suspended from a silvered Chinese dragon, and with six further dragons on the chandelier itself each of which supported a lotus-shaped shade. The whole was hung with innumerable cut-glass drops, measured some thirty feet in height and weighed about a ton. When it was installed in 1817 the cost was over £5,000. It was taken down in 1834, after the death of George IV, because it was said that King William 'was fearful lest, from its immense weight, the supports should give way and some fatal accident occur'. It was rehung at a later date, and remains in the room today.

In the same building, in the Music Room, the Prince Regent placed 'a very beautiful lustre of cut glass, designed in the pagoda style, and sustaining by its chain-work an immense lamp in the form of the nelumbrium, or water-lily. The upper leaves are of white ground glass, edged with gold, and enriched with transparent devices derived from the mythology of the Chinese; the lower leaves are of a pale crimson hue. At the bottom are golden dragons in attitudes of flight.' Eight smaller lamps, to a similar design, were also in the room, and in the words of a writer of the time 'adding greatly to the general effect when illumined for evening parties'. They cost a total of £4,290 12*s*. The centre chandelier and five of the smaller ones remain still in the Music Room; three of the latter are now in Buckingham Palace, but copies complete the set at Brighton.

In the Victorian age metal again came to the fore. At the 1851 Great Exhibition R. W. Winfield of Birmingham and

London showed two chandeliers illustrated in colour in the official catalogue. They were described briefly as follows: 'Bronzed gas chandelier in the Elizabethan style, with ornamental enamelled shades', and 'Gas chandelier with birds and figures'. The first has the central column decorated with Italian renaissance-style scrollwork with male and female heads in relief, and the six arms are in the form of winged animals with the 'ornamental enamelled shades' rising from their heads. The second of the chandeliers is in gilt metal and has figures of children, naked except for a little discreet draping, seated on garlands beneath a circular trelliswork canopy on which are birds; the straight shaft is partly concealed by metal lilies and leaves and is encircled by birds on the wing; and the six curved arms are fitted with etched glass shades.

Chestnut roasters. The chestnut roaster is a small brass box with a hinged cover, on the end of a handle about two feet long. The sides of the box are pierced and sometimes also the cover, which usually has a small additional handle by which to open it.

Few of the surviving examples of roasters belong to a period earlier than that of Queen Victoria, although most of them are claimed to be much older. There seems to be no reason why they should have been as popular in the past as the number of alleged old roasters seems to indicate, and it may be assumed, perhaps, that the idea of a nation of nut-eating eighteenth-century Englishmen is a comparatively modern one.

Clocks. *See* **Scientific Instruments.**

Coal scuttles. With the coming into wide use of coal as a household fuel in the early years of the eighteenth century, it was found convenient to have a supply handy by the fireside. It is recorded that in 1715 Lady Grissell Baillie spent the sum of 21*s* 6*d* on the purchase of 'a coper scuttel'. This one, along with others of the time, is no longer to be seen; the wear-and-tear of daily use made them expendable articles.

Surviving scuttles rarely can be dated to before the second half of the nineteenth century.

Two of the most popular shapes are known as the 'Helmet'; which resembles an inverted helmet, and what may be called the 'Shovel' shape. At the 1851 Exhibition Messrs Tylor and Sons, of London, showed 'A copper coal scuttle

Figure 4. A helmet-shaped coal-scuttle (left) and (right) a pattern shown at the 1851 Great Exhibition.

of new and simple design'. Another display by the same firm is entered in the catalogue as: 'Copper coal scoops, exhibiting the changes in their patterns during the last 70 years.' Also at the Exhibition was an ingenious accessory described as follows: 'Registered ornamental and self-supplying pedestal coal vase, presenting for use only sufficient coals to charge the hand scoop, when a fresh supply is given from the upper chamber.' No examples of this appear to have survived the past 110 years.

A use as a coal-container has been found in recent years for articles of antique pattern intended by their makers for entirely different purposes. An instance is the copper and brass milk pail, imported once from Holland in large numbers, but now made in England to the same design. No longer is it intended for the dairy, and many who use them for coal are unaware of the purpose of the originals.

Curfews. The curfew is a semi-circular domed cover made of brass or copper, and gets its name from the French, *couvre-feu*: fire-cover. It was so-called by an eighteenth-century collector, a Mr Gostling of Canterbury, who had one and thought it was used for extinguishing a fire in response to the ringing of a curfew bell. In fact the Curfew was used to cover the embers of a wood fire at night to prevent air from reaching them. In the morning, the embers would be raked, and a few puffs from a bellows would get a blaze restarted.

Although examples of eighteenth-century date, and perhaps earlier, are to be found occasionally in England, it is doubtful whether they were made in that country. More probably they originated in the Netherlands.

Curtain-holders. The curtain-holder, known sometimes as a *Hold-back*, came into use about the middle of the eighteenth century. Made usually of gilt brass it took at least two forms: one was a large-sized clip, and the other a short steel rod with a large gilt-metal ornament at the end. Its function was to retain the drawn curtain in place at the side of a window, and it was used normally in pairs.

Simple in design at first, they grew more elaborate in Regency times, and by the year of the Great Exhibition their patterns were as complicated as those of other metal products of the period.

Door knockers. Many of the great cathedrals and churches of medieval times had on their principal door a lion's head, more or less recognizable as such, with a large ring in its mouth. The origin and purpose of these has caused argument ever since as there is no evidence of their use other than for decoration. They are not knockers in the accepted sense, for there is no boss against which the ring can be hit, and most of them are placed in such a position as to be useless in helping to open or close the door. The only explanation would seem to be the traditional one: that they gave the right of sanctuary to anyone who held the ring. Whether innocent or guilty, a man holding the ring might not be hacked to pieces or arrested by a pursuing mob of soldiers or civilians.

Having gained the safety of the Sanctuary, either by grasping a ring, or in some instances, sitting on a special stool, the felon usually had to confess his crime to one of the clergy, pay a fee of admission to a religious house, and at Durham he had to toll a special bell and wear a gown of sack-cloth. With all these conditions to be observed it is perhaps understandable that the custom has fallen into disuse.

In England brass door knockers on houses became a common sight during the course of the eighteenth century, when the building of towns was taking place on a large scale. The designs, on the whole, were neither varied nor inspired, and the article was primarily functional. Most of the patterns current at that time have remained in production ever since, and it is sometimes not easy to distinguish old from new. Adam-style knockers, incorporating Classical motifs, particularly rams' heads, husks and urns; dolphins; and clenched fists remain as popular today as when they were first introduced.

Miniature knockers, designed for the doors of rooms within the house, are plentiful but are not old. The majority of them, when examined carefully, will be found to display no signs of age in spite of their makers' predeliction for 'ye olde worlde' in design.

Today when the knocker is more ornamental than anything else, it may be of interest to read the following extract from a book published more than 100 years ago: in 1853. It is taken from Max Schlesinger's *Saunterings in and about London*, and describes humorously, with perhaps a deal of truth as well, the significance of the door knocker at that time:

'We now approach the street-door, and put the knocker in motion. Do not fancy that this is an easy process. It is by far easier to learn the language of Englishmen than to learn the language of the knocker; and many strangers protest that a knocker is the most difficult of all musical instruments.

'It requires a good ear and a skilful hand to make yourself understood and to escape remarks and ridicule. Every class of society announces itself at the gate of the fortress by means of the rhythm of the knocker. The postman gives two loud raps in quick succession; and for the visitor a gentle but peremptory *tremolo* is *de rigeur*. The master of the house gives a *tremolo crescendo*, and the servant who announces his master, turns the knocker into a battering-ram, and plies it with such goodwill that the house shakes to its foundations. Tradesmen, on the other hand, butchers, milkmen, bakers, and greengrocers, are not allowed to touch the knockers—they ring a bell which communicates with the kitchen.

'All this is very easy in theory but very difficult in practice. Bold, and otherwise inexperienced, strangers believe that they assert their dignity, if they move the knocker with conscious energy. Vain delusion! They are mistaken for footmen. Modest people, on the contrary are treated as mendicants. The middle course, in this, as in other respects, is most difficult.

'Two different motives are assigned for this custom. Those who dislike England on principle, and according to whom the very dogs are an aristocratic abuse, assert that the various ways of plying the knocker are most intimately connected with the prejudices of caste. Others again say, that the arrangement is conductive to comfort, since the inmates of the house know at once what sort of visitor is desiring admittance.'

Whereas the electric bell offers some chances for the assertion of individuality, the length of the ring or the sequence of dots and dashes, the twentieth-century automatic two-tone variety has finally killed all efforts of that nature.

Douters, Extinguishers and Snuffers. *Douters* are like

small pairs of scissors in appearance, and their 'blades' have rounded flat discs between which the wick can be gripped and the flame extinguished. The virtue in using Douters lies in the fact that no evil-smelling smoke is given off in the process.

Extinguishers are conical in shape, and have either a curled handle or a shaped arm by which they can be replaced on the candle-holder after use. Almost all Chamber Candlesticks have a bracket for holding an extinguisher, which is often referred to in error as a Snuffer.

Snuffers: the eighteenth-century tallow candle was made with a twisted cotton wick that bent over as it burned, came into contact with the edge of the candle where it made an unsightly, and often dangerous, mess. At the same time it gave very little light, emitted black smoke and an unpleasant smell. These shortcomings were avoidable by the frequent use of a pair of snuffers: a scissors-like device, with a small box fitted half-way along the blades, that trimmed the wick and left it of sufficient length to burn brightly, but not long enough to bend over.

The wax candle did not have these serious defects and could be left to burn free from attention. It was, however, a much more costly article, and could only be relied on to be trouble-free when it had been made carefully with the thickness of wick matched to the diameter of the candle. Otherwise, results not dissimilar to those from tallow could be expected to follow.

Snuffers were made of brass in the first half of the eighteenth century. They were usually complete with a stand in which they rested when not in use, and this is usually an oblong container raised on a column and domed foot. Sets of brass snuffers and stands are rare, and few of the existing examples are genuinely of the period to which they are ascribed.

The use for snuffers ceased when a Frenchman named Cambacères introduced a plaited wick in 1820. This, when used in combination with the newly-discovered stearine wax proved to be self-consuming, and snuffers went into retirement.

Engravers' plates. Engraving was the most important method of illustrating books and reproducing likenesses of people and objects available during the eighteenth century. For the purpose, whichever of the various processes was employed, a copper plate was the first requirement. This had to be of extreme smoothness, and its preparation was a skilled and lengthy business.

A contemporary account gives a very good idea of the work involved. After referring to the care needed in selecting a suitably ductile grade of copper, 'free from any veins, specks, or dissimilar parts, but of an equal texture through the whole', the writer continued as follows:

'The copper being chosen, it must be fabricated into plates of the size demanded, the thickness of which may be in proportion of a line to plates that are a foot by nine inches. These plates must then be well forged and planished by a brazier; which should be done cold: for by managing this operation well, the porosity of the copper may be greatly removed, which is for the most obvious reasons of great consequence. When a plate is forged it should be examined which side is the most even, and the least flawed or cracked; and then the polishing may be thus performed.

'Put the plate upon a board leaning obliquely, and in the bottom of which two nails or points are fixed, to keep it from sliding off; and then take a large piece of grind-stone dipped in water, and rub it very strongly once in every part lengthways, and then the same breadthways, keeping it moist with water; and repeat this operation until no hollows appear, nor the least mark made by the hammer in forging, or any other flaws, holes, or inequalities. After this take a piece of good pumice-stone, and rub the plate with it in the same manner as was done before with the grind-stone, till all the scratches and marks made of the grind-stone may, by the pumice-stone, be likewise taken away, and then wash it thoroughly clean. The scratches and marks of the pumice-stone should then be taken out by rubbing the plate in the same manner with a piece of oil-stone, till all the marks and scorings of the pumice-stone be taken out: and the plate should be then washed with water till it be perfectly clean.'

Following these three treatments with diminishing coarsenesses of stone, a fourth polishing is given by rubbing with a stick of charcoal. 'The plate being brought to this state, the polishing must be finished with a steel burnisher, with which it must be strongly rubbed; the best method of moving the burnisher is not to move it lengthways, or breadthways, but in a diagonal direction, or from corner to corner, which will more effectually take out all remains of the former scorings or lines. The copper must be thus burnished till it be as bright as a looking-glass in every part; but if, when the rest is thus bright, some particular spots appear dull, or that any lines remain, such faults should be again worked with the burnisher, till the whole be uniformly shining.'

The actual processes of engraving: line, dry-point, mezzotint, etching, and stipple, are outside the scope of this volume. All were carried out with carefully-prepared copper plates, of which the making was a skilled and busy craft throughout the eighteenth century.

Escutcheons. The ornament round the keyhole on a piece of furniture which was placed there not only for decoration, but to prevent wear-and-tear that would otherwise take place. Brass escutcheons were in use from late in the seventeenth century, and most of the English ones were cast with raised ornament. Others were flat and shaped plates, patterned with punched lines and circles. In the eighteenth century more flamboyant examples were designed and illustrated by Chippendale in his *Director*, and these were finished with gilding to prevent tarnish as much as to enhance their appearance. Later, escutcheons were stamped from thin brass plate and were mostly of simple outline.

A form of escutcheon used from the mid-eighteenth century is a simple brass frame of a shape to take the key, and placed by the cabinet-maker in the keyhole cut in the woodwork. Early ones often had a raised and curved edge, but later examples fitted flush with the surface. Old escutcheons of this type have the lower, narrow, edge made with a slight curve. Modern ones are quite straight.

French and other continental escutcheons in the eighteenth century were made of gilt brass or bronze, and their design followed prevailing fashions.

Ewers and Jugs. Before the days when water came through a pipe and out of a tap it was more highly valued than it is today, and containers for it were treated with the importance they then deserved. Ewers and jugs were the principal water holders in houses or public buildings, and in one form or another have been in use for many centuries.

According to Dr Johnson a ewer is 'a vessel in which water is brought for washing the hands', and jug is 'a large drinking vessel with a gibbous or swelling belly'. In the last two hundred years many words have changed their meanings and the *Oxford Dictionary* now says that a ewer is 'used to bring water for washing the hands', but that a jug is 'a deep vessel for holding liquids', without specifying whether for drinking, washing, or for any other purpose. In the twentieth century the word ewer has fallen largely out of use, and in the United States and elsewhere a jug is referred to as a pitcher.

At this distance of time it is often difficult or impossible to be certain whether an old vessel was for drinking water or washing water, but it seems that the aquamanile (the word meaning literally 'hand washer'), dealt with earlier in this book, was used for the latter purpose. It was essential at the dining-table for washing the hands between courses before forks came into use.

Long-spouted ewers of brass, on tall feet, elaborately decorated with silver inlay, were made in the thirteenth century in many countries ranging from Persia to Venice. Farther to the west, on the mainland of Europe and in the British Isles, less highly ornamented ones were made. Some of these are cast with inscriptions and coats-of-arms in relief, and are not dissimilar in this respect to mortars and bells made at about the same period. One of the ewers of this type, in the Victoria and Albert Museum, bears the royal arms of England and was made in the late fourteenth century. Another of about the same date, now in the British Museum, was found in Kumasi, on the Gold Coast of Africa, in 1896, although it is not now known how it reached there.

The Italian bronze casters of the late sixteenth century were responsible for some interesting, and very rare, ewers. Typical of them is one in the form of a grotesque monster seated with its head tilted back and mouth wide open, its hair streams back and merges into a handle so that it can be used readily.

In the eighteenth and nineteenth centuries ewers were made in England and elsewhere from sheet copper and sheet brass, but continual use has taken a heavy toll and few of the surviving examples are very old.

Extinguishers. *See* **Douters.**

Fenders and Grates. When coal, often known in the seventeenth and eighteenth centuries as 'sea coal' because it was almost invariably brought to London and other places by boat, replaced wood as the national fuel, the grate took possession of the fireplace from andirons. Logs needed support occasionally, but lumps of coal had to be held together in some type of basket so that the flame could spread from piece to piece. Also, more than wood it needed raising so that a draught of air could help it to burn.

The earliest grates were made entirely of iron and with the minimum of decoration. By about 1730, after there had been a period of moulded ornament, polished pierced and engraved steel facings were often applied to the front of the utilitarian basket to make it look more attractive. Later in the century, brass was added in the same way: the front frieze or apron and the corner uprights being the usual places for ornament. Although when clean and shining they must have looked very handsome in the sparkle of the flames, smoke and heat must have dirtied them quickly and made upkeep a daily routine.

On rare occasions the Chinese alloy, paktong, was used in the same manner as brass or steel, and had the advantage of tarnishing less quickly. A visitor to Fawley Court, Buckinghamshire, in 1771 commented on the new interior decorations in the house, and mentioned that the owner 'has laid out £8,000, I believe'. In the drawing-room, 'fitted up with every possible elegance of the present taste', was a paktong grate which cost 100 guineas.

Brass was a more suitable metal for fenders than for grates; placed at some distance from the source of heat the metal would not be dirtied so quickly. Although fenders were used occasionally with wood fires to restrain flying sparks, their use spread rapidly with the introduction of coal-burning in a raised grate when falling embers might be a danger. The earliest examples were of steel, pierced and engraved, and usually repeating the design of the steel frieze on the grate. If the grate was of brass, the fender would be made of the same metal, and matching also in pattern.

Most eighteenth-century fenders measured little more than a few inches in height, and the later examples had a base of thin sheet iron to keep them rigid. They varied in shape, and examples can be found that are bowed, serpentine or perfectly straight. The lower edge of the front was usually a cast moulding of metal fixed to the upright part to keep the whole steady.

In the course of the nineteenth century the fender grew taller. Often it was fitted with cast brass feet in the shape of lions' paws, and some examples have uprights at either end against which fire-irons can be rested. The 1851 Exhibition saw a number of fenders, including one described as 'Chased fender, in ormolu; consisting of dogs, stags and foliage'. This particular example was made in a complex pattern of dogs chasing stags among curlicues and foliage, and although decorative it was so much pierced that it would perhaps not have been very effective in use.

Fire-dogs. *See* **Andirons.**

Fire-irons. The majority of English eighteenth-century fire-irons, sets of implements including shovel, poker and tongs, were made of polished steel. Some examples have copper or brass ornament in the form of finials to the handles, but usually they are of steel throughout. Occasionally, sets are met with made entirely of brass, but most of them are either of continental origin or are later in date. English-made brass fire-irons were very popular in the Victorian age, and most surviving examples, in spite of the fact that they appear to be of earlier design and manufacture, are no more than a hundred years old.

Footman. A type of trivet supported on four tall legs, and usually with a shaped hole in the top for lifting it. While some were made of iron there are many old examples of brass ornamented with piercing and engraving.

Forks. These were in use in Italy in the sixteenth century, and travellers who returned to England made much play on the unusual custom. One writer explained to his readers, that 'The reason for this curiosity is because the Italian cannot endure by any means to have his dish touched by fingers, seeing that all men's fingers are not alike clean.' Forks had been used in England at that date, but only for special purposes; such as one described in 1463 as being for eating 'grene Gynger', and another belonging to the Royal Plate of Queen Elizabeth I listed as 'a ginger forke'. As la as 1824 a London silversmith recorded in his autobiography how one of his clients had invited him to dinner at a fashionable hotel. He refused, and his host asked why he had done so: 'Because,' said he, taking up one of the silver forks, 'I know how to sell these articles, but not how to use them.'

While their personal use outside Italy was rare in Europe until the seventeenth century, forks were employed earlier for holding a joint of meat while it was being carved and for serving. For these purposes the twin prongs of early specimens were sharply pointed, and it has been suggested that for this reason their widespread adoption was delayed. In due course, when the prongs were left blunt, as they are today, there was less danger of the diner drawing his own blood during a meal.

It is not surprising, therefore, that genuine old forks are very rare. A latten or brass one, excavated in London but not necessarily of English make, dating from the fifteenth/sixteenth century has been recorded.

Frames. Rectangular, oval and round frames for small pictures, silhouettes, etc., were made in England in the last quarter of the eighteenth century. They were often of pearwood covered with stamped brass, patterned and lacquered to resemble carved and gilded wood. They must have been cheap to produce in quantity compared with the cost of the article they imitate. Small frames of solid cast brass were made in the same period in both England and other countries.

Gongs. Gongs originated in the Far East, and are made from bronze treated in such a manner that it can be hammered to the required shape, size and thickness and then hardened to produce its typical vibrant sound. The circular gong with a raised rim, suspended usually from a heavily-carved blackwood stand, was not uncommon as a feature of Edwardian and Victorian homes in England. It is now seldom seen or heard.

Some varieties of Chinese and Japanese gongs are not always recognizable immediately for what they really are. Made from flat and thick pieces of bronze, they are usually moulded with decoration and inscribed; the inscription often giving details of the donor, the place to which given, and the date of presentation. They were hung outside temples and beaten to summon the faithful to prayer. A number of them have been brought to Europe and America from the Orient, and remain silent in museums.

Grates. *See* **Fenders.**

Horns. The first horns were taken from dead animals, and when the point had been broken off it was found that blowing produced one or more notes—'barely approximating to musical sounds'. Horns of bronze are of ancient date and were used for the rallying of people either for battle, or for more peaceful purposes. Bronze Age horns have been excavated in various parts of Europe, and a writer of about 1700 recorded the following about an unusual number of them discovered in Ireland:

'There were 8 trumpets, 4 of one make and 4 of another, found in the lower Barony of Dungannon about 7 years ago. Two I have by me, they are of cast brass about the thickness of an English half-crown.

'The first is 24 inches long according to the turn or arch it makes, and is three inches in diameter at the large end, and at the small end it is solid for about 2 inches, with a loop at top to hang it by, and another loop between the solid part and the mouth-piece. The mouth-piece is oval 5 inches from the solid end, $1\frac{3}{4}$ inches long and 1 inch wide: the sides are smooth, round and even, easy for the lips of a man, but will not admit of any sound by blast as a horn does, but by the articulate voice of tooting it will. One may raise his voice in it to the highest pitch, and bring it to the deepest bass.

'The other is 26 inches long, one inch wide at the small

end and three inches at the other; but seems to be imperfect for want of a mouth-piece, the small end seems to be fitted to receive one. On the back there is a hole, and another under the moulding. The first I believe was to fasten the mouth-piece, the second I imagine was to stop or open with the finger to alter the sound at pleasure.'

Curved horns of this type, usually with one or more bands of moulded ornament at the wider end, are rare, and mostly to be found in museums. Specimens of later date are to be found at Winchester, in the City Museum, and at Dover, Kent; the latter still in use at Mayoral elections.

A very fine copper horn enamelled in colours at Limoges by Leonard Limousin in the sixteenth century, was made in four sections joined together by narrow bands of silver. More a work of art than a practical hunting-horn, it belonged once to Horace Walpole, the eighteenth-century collector, and when his treasures were sold many years after his death, in 1842, it fetched 125 guineas. Exactly fifty years later it was re-sold at Christies', and bought by a member of the Rothschild family for the sum of 6,300 guineas.

Horse brasses. The history of the horse brass goes back a long way in time, and from a mention in the Bible of 'ornaments on camel's necks' it can be assumed that ornaments were worn also by horses in Old Testament days. It has been thought that amongst the earliest of European horse decorations were small bronze or brass plaques enamelled or engraved with the coat-of-arms of the owner, or of the reigning monarch, worn on the harness of a war horse. From this, it is conjectured further, grew the custom of decorating animals having less exalted ownership with more commonplace motifs. Many of the brasses were sold at fairs by hawkers, and their designs would naturally be of such a nature as to appeal to their customers. Adaptations of inn signs and of popular heraldic devices, barrels or other objects that showed the trade of the owner, and trees and flowers of the countryside, are among the two thousand or so designs recorded as current at one time or another.

The complete regalia of brasses borne by a fully-equipped cart horse totals some six to seven pounds in weight; no slight burden. It comprises some or all of the following pieces, with or without modifications or additions to suit the taste and purse of the owner of the animal, and the importance of the occasion:

Face Brasses: one or more to hang down over the forehead.
Two Ear Brasses: one behind each ear.
Six Runner Brasses: three at each side of the runners at the shoulders.
Six to ten Martingale Brasses: the martingale is a strap hanging down from the horse's collar and fixed to the girth between the forelegs.

In addition there can be any number of brass rosettes and other shaped ornaments, together with *Noseband Plates* and *Name Plates*.

A Flyer (known also as a *swinger*, or a *Fly Terret*): a miniature brass swinging loosely in a frame and fixed over the head of the animal. Some of the Flyers have a small bell, and others are mounted with a brush strikingly coloured in red, white and blue.

A set of Bells: often in four tiers, consisting of The Lead with five bells, The Lash with four, The Body with three, and The Thill also with three. Each of the tiers sounds its own chord, and while it has been said that they were worn to drive away evil spirits, it is equally probable they were used to give warning of approach in narrow lanes and at night.

Hames: curved horn-shaped brass pieces affixed to each side of the collar

Much has been written about the significance of the various patterns of horse brasses, and many writers have attempted to sustain the theory that their basic designs go back to the days of sun worship and the general celebration of pagan rites. Whether this is so or not will continue to be argued, but it is clearly understandable that a man should make the most of the appearance of his most valuable working-ally. This would have been the case especially on days of celebration and display, and it remains the same even now. The annual parades of cart and van horses, held still in London but with fast-diminishing numbers of entrants, show

Figure 5.

the animals bedecked in all the finery, suitable or incongruous, that their proud owners can provide. The fact that many of the brass ornaments, gleaming as their bearers move, are circular in shape is equally likely because a round convex disc is a good reflector, as because it resembles the sun in appearance.

Here, alphabetically, are brief notes on some of the patterns:

Anchor: symbol of St Nicholas, the patron saint of sailors, travellers and children, and used on brasses for horses working in docks and by canals.
Barrel: one or more barrels, or tuns, were used on brasses for horses pulling brewery drays.
Bell: apart from the possibility that a well-polished bell might ward off the glance of an 'evil eye', the bell was used on a brass perhaps because The Bell, a highly popular name for public houses, was the favourite inn of the owner. Other

inn signs that were adopted as horse brasses include the Boar, the Mitre, the Swan, and the Wheatsheaf.

Carter: one design shows a carter asleep on his wagon, and another shows the same man vigilant and driving his horse.

Churn: made for use on animals drawing dairy vehicles.

Crescent: a crescent was said to have been a most powerful protection against the 'evil eye'. A horseshoe is said still to bring good luck to the finder, and the superstition of hanging them with the points upwards has been current for many centuries. The ornaments taken by Gideon from the necks of the camels of Zebah and Zulmunna were described as being 'like the waning moon', so there would seem to be historical and mythological precedents for the use of crescent- or horseshoe-shaped brasses. They are probably the most plentiful, and are found incorporated with other emblems or on their own.

Dog: various dogs are found represented on brasses, but most are of modern manufacture.

Eagle: this and other birds are featured, but the American eagle must be treated with suspicion on account of its probable lack of age.

Engine: a railway engine was on brasses made perhaps for use on the horses employed by railway companies.

Flags: both English and French flags are shown on brasses made in the last years of the nineteenth century.

Heart: brasses were made either of heart-shaped outline or incorporating one or more hearts in their pattern, forming an amulet that is said to ensure long life to the bearer.

Lion: a symbol of strength, fortitude and majesty—not inappropriate to the Shire horse.

Peacock: a bird sacred to the Greek goddess of fertility, Hera, and brasses bearing it were used fittingly to decorate brood mares.

Thistle: the emblem of Scotland, and produced doubtless for wearing north of the Border or for the animals of those who had emigrated south.

Windmill: there are several variations of this design. Doubtless, they were worn on horses owned by millers, and where windmills were a familiar feature of the local scenery. It is said that the pattern was once found frequently in Lincolnshire.

The use of horse brasses in England did not become general until some time in the nineteenth century, and only a very few genuine ones of earlier date are in existence. The majority of surviving specimens are about a hundred years old, or less. There are many varieties showing the head of Queen Victoria, some of which commemorate the Jubilee of 1897, and others show Edward VII, both as Prince of Wales and as King, George V, Edward VIII and George VI. Others commemorate politicians, generals, jockeys, and poets, and there are brasses of recent make with portraits of Sir Winston Churchill and Field-Marshal Lord Montgomery.

Although they are certainly not exclusive to England, whence they were introduced probably from the East, it is the horse brasses of that country that have received the most attention. Several books and many magazine articles have been published on them in the past thirty years, and a number of large collections have been formed. To assuage the thirst of eager collectors many new designs of brasses have been issued, and old ones carefully reproduced. The signs of age and wear found on old specimens have been copied with varying success, but most modern ones show few traces of any real desire to deceive. As horse brasses are sold comparatively cheaply it is seldom a paying proposition to fake them with any thoroughness; a process that must take time as well as skill, and would bring only a slight reward in terms of cash. On the whole, keen collectors are interested in old brasses that have been in actual use, and bear genuine signs of wear. They were more carefully finished by hand than are their modern counterparts, but sand-blasting and acid baths go quite a long way in deceiving the unwary.

Inlay. Furniture inlaid with brass was probably first made in Italy, but reached its greatest and most characteristic elaboration in France, where André Charles Boulle (1642–1732) gave his name to an inlay combining metal and tortoiseshell. Boulle's inlaid pieces were veneered in an ingenious manner: thin sheets of tortoiseshell and brass were set on one another, a drawn pattern placed on top and the pattern cut through the layers with a fine saw. The result was a jig-saw of pieces; in one instance with a background of metal, and in the other with one of tortoiseshell. These are known as *première partie* and *contre partie* (first part and counter-part), and a pair of pieces of furniture was often made, matching in design but with one of each type of veneer.

Boulle was known as the most skilful of Paris cabinet-makers before he reached the age of thirty, and in 1672 he was granted a workshop in the Louvre under the patronage of Louis XIV. Once he had achieved fame by his skilful handling of marquetry, and in particular that of brass and tortoiseshell, he did not vary his style throughout his long life. Four of his seven sons followed in the footsteps of their father, and continued making furniture in a similar manner until the last of them died in 1754.

Although there were no successors in name, there were plenty in manner. Boulle, in the style of the master, continued to be made for the rest of the eighteenth century and throughout the nineteenth. All these pieces, made during a period of two centuries, are referred to generally as 'Boulle', and the fact that André Charles did not sign his work makes identification of pieces from his workshop even harder. Two chests of drawers made in 1708–9 and for which a payment was made of 3,000 livres, now at Versailles, are fully authenticated, and perhaps a further twenty pieces are attributable to him with good reason.

Early in the nineteenth century there was a revival of inlaying in brass, and plain mahogany furniture of dark colour was relieved with lines of brass bordering the edges, and in other suitable places.

The work of Boulle had a slight influence in England. An inventory of the contents of Kensington Palace taken in 1679 lists tables and other articles, the frames all inlaid with metal, 'bespoke by the Queen and came in after her death from Mr Johnson'. There is also a piece now at Windsor Castle which is almost certainly a 'fine writing-desk inlaid with metall' which Johnson (or Jensen to use his alternative name) supplied in 1695.

In the middle years of the eighteenth century, several emigrant cabinet-makers from France worked in England and, not unnaturally, sought to make furniture in their native manner. One of them, Peter Langlois of Tottenham Court Road, had a bi-lingual trade-card, announcing in both English and French that he 'Makes all sorts of fine cabinets and commodes, made and inlaid in the politest manner with brass and tortoiseshell'. An entry in a Directory of 1763 states that 'This artist performs all sorts of curious Inlaid Work, particularly Commodes in the foreign taste inlaid with tortoiseshell, Brass, etc.'

Another foreigner was Abraham Roentgen, born in Germany, but working in England during the years 1731 to 1738. Some mahogany tea-tables on plain three-legged bases inlaid with engraved brass on the knees of the base and on the top, have been attributed to him.

At the same time as the revival of simple brass inlaying in France, a similar revival took place in England. Chairs, tables and other pieces were embellished with brass, mostly in the form of straight lines but sometimes stars and more elaborate patterns. This use of shining metal against mahogany or rosewood is a hallmark of Regency furniture, which is rarely absent in pieces of better quality.

Jugs. *See* **Ewers.**

Kettles. The kettle grew up with the teapot; the use of the one called for the other. Tea, which had started to become popular about the end of the seventeenth century, was expensive, and was treated in a manner reflecting its high cost. The teapot was noticeably of a small size, and the minimum quantity of leaf was used to gain the greatest amount of liquid. The teapot, therefore, was refilled frequently with hot water, and a kettle which was raised on a small stand with a heating-lamp underneath it, was always present at the tea-table. Although silver kettles were available for the wealthy, the greater number of homes had them of copper.

A newspaper advertisement from *The Daily Advertiser* of 12th November, 1741, gives a description of what was in use at the time. It reads as follows:

> 'To be sold by William Heath (brother to George Heath, the original maker, from Kingsgate Street, Holborn) at the third house above Forrest's Coffee House, opposite the Mews Gate, Charing Cross. A parcel of curious copper brown Tea-kettles and lamps, the colour of brown china burnt in after the India manner, which for curious work and colour exceed any that come from Holland or any other place. They want no other cleaning than to be wiped with a dry cloth, and the colour will be always the same. The great demand there has been for the above maker's work is a sufficient proof that they exceed any Dutch, and give a general satisfaction. Those gentlemen and ladies who are pleased to favour me with their orders may now be supplied with great choice of the above goods in the newest fashions, all warranted as usual, and sold at no more than the following prices: Three-pint tea-kettles and lamps at 10*s*. Two-quart ditto at 13*s*. Likewise several other sorts of curious work in the above colour, all warranted to be made by the above maker and original inventor, George Heath, having engaged him and the best

workmen in London, who by me are only employed; and sold at little more than prime cost.

'Note. There is just finished by the above maker, and of the same colour, a parcel of curious steak-dishes and lamps, tea-pots and coffee-pots, the insides lined with block tin.'

The most popular early teapot was made of Yi-hsing stoneware of a rich red-brown colour, and this quickly gained a reputation for brewing the best tea. Sent over with the leaf from China, the teapots were imitated in Europe; in Germany at Meissen (Dresden), in England by various Staffordshire makers, and in Holland by a potter named de Milde. It is to these that the advertiser refers in speaking of 'brown china burnt in after the India manner'; the latter phrase meaning with the colouring baked into the ware in the Chinese way. The fact that Chinese porcelain came to the West in the ships of the East India Companies led to popular confusion, and frequently it was called 'Indian' in error.

The earliest silver tea-kettle so far recorded is dated 1694, and is in the Norwich Castle Museum. It is not improbable that copper examples were made from about the same time or even slightly earlier, for there is a reference to a silver one in 1687. Surviving copper specimens of before 1800, in spite of the frequency with which all and sundry are labelled 'eighteenth century' are understandably very rare. They were made for daily use, and received it. In spite of the fact that they were carefully made by hand the weight of metal employed was limited by their purpose: no one would want one so strong and heavily constructed that it could not be lifted, and their life was comparatively hard-working and short.

The majority of kettles to be found are of nineteenth century date, although many show Georgian characteristics. Being an article of daily use their design remained more or less unchanged over the centuries, and the same patterns were used for about two hundred years. This is not unreasonable when it is considered that the original designs were of such merit that little could be changed to improve them.

Brass tea-kettles on stands were made in the late nineteenth century and these, like the copper ones, are of patterns reminiscent of Georgian times.

Knockers. *See* **Door knockers.**

Lamps. The oldest method of lighting, and at the same time the simplest, was by the use of a wick in a bowl of oil. This dates back to prehistoric days, and can still be found in use in some of the more remote and less civilized parts of the globe. At first of clay, these oil containers were made later from metal, and an Egyptian specimen in copper, dating from about 3,000 B.C., is in the Louvre, Paris. It is raised on a circular domed foot, and the basin or dish has the usual spout in which the wick rested.

In Greek and Roman times, although the majority of lamps were of baked clay, many were made of bronze and some had places for more than a single wick. The basic design remained unchanged, except that the open grooved spout became a covered projection with a hole from which the wick projected. Roman bronze lamps made for the wealthier inhabitants of the cities were often ornamented with elaborate patterns, in contrast to the purely functional appearance of cheaper pottery examples. Specimens made probably for use in temples for the worship of the God Priapus often show considerable ingenuity in their design.

A vairant of these lamps is the type known in Scotland as a *crusie*, in Cornwall as a *chill*, and in the Channel Islands as a *crasset*. The clay-bodied lamp left traces of oil where it had been standing but the double-panned crusie, even if it smelled and smoked, did not normally make a mess. The pans are known as Valves, and were made by hammering a piece of metal over a 'master' shape or die.

The upper valve of the crusie is no more than the old open basin lamp of prehistoric times, but below hangs a further valve to catch drips and the whole thing suspends by a hook for hanging from a shelf or anything handy. The upper valve usually adjusts so that the oil can be made to run towards the wick.

Double-valve lamps are seldom older than the seventeenth century, and in the course of time were made in every country of Europe. Later and more sophisticated versions

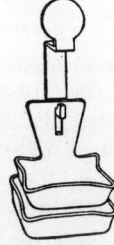

Figure 6. A Cornish copper 'Chill'.

had covered pans with a short protruding tube for the wick, and this is the type usually found in the United States. All of these lamps were made of iron, but brass and copper were used also. Local variations in design were numerous, and Scottish examples usually have a pair of prominent curled 'ears' of metal on either side of the suspending handle of the upper valve.

Mention should be made of a type of continental brass lamp of the seventeenth and eighteenth centuries that is still seen often in antique shops. It stands on a column support and has spouts for three or more wicks round the bulbous oil container. This is hung about with a number of implements for maintaining the light: suspended from chains are such things as spikes and tweezers for handling the wicks, extinguishers, metal reflecting plates, small buckets to hold fragments of charred wick, and pairs of scissor-like douters to put out the flame without causing smoke and smell.

A great step forward in artificial lighting that took place

was due to the invention in about 1782 of a new type of lamp by a Swiss, Ami Argand of Geneva. He devised a tubular wick rising between two tubes, the inner of them allowing air to reach the inside of the flame, and to this was added a shaped glass shade, which also aided combustion. Only fish or vegetable oils were available for use in any lamps at the time, and in spite of the probability that their presence would be detected at a distance, and not by their light alone, they became very popular.

Argand made an initial attempt to launch his invention in France, but was not immediately successful. A man named Quinquet marketed a close imitation of the lamp, and examples of them, although rightly called 'Argands' in other countries are called 'Quinquets' in France. In London Ami Argand's invention had a much better reception; he visited the city in 1784, obtained a patent and arranged for manufacture by Matthew Boulton. Within two years his lamps had become commonplace, and were widely copied after his patent had been declared invalid at law. A German visitor in 1786, Sophie von La Roche, noted on a visit she paid to Sadler's Wells, then on the green outskirts of London:

> 'We were astonished at the handsome building and illumination of the hall, consisting of some hundred splendid Argand lamps which were bright as sunlight, and proved at the same time that such lamps do not smoke one little bit'.

Again, in Oxford Street at night, she commented:

> 'Most of all we admired a stall with Argand and other lamps, situated in a corner-house, and forming a really dazzling spectacle; every variety of lamp, crystal, lacquer and metal ones, silver and brass in every possible shade; large and small lamps arranged so artistically and so beautifully lit, that each was visible as in broad daylight. There were reflecting lamps inside, which intensified the

glare to such an extent that my eye could scarce stand it a moment: large pewter oil-vessels, gleaming like silver, were ranged there, and oil of every description, so that the lamp and the oil can be bought and taken home together if one likes, the oil in a beautiful glass flask, and the wick, too, in a dainty box. The highest lord and humble labourer may purchase here lamps of immense beauty and price or at a very reasonable figure, and both receive equally rapid and courteous attention. I stayed long enough to notice this, and was pleased with a system which supplied the common need—light—in this spot, whether for guineas or for pence, so efficiently.'

The large-sized wick of the Argand lamp was greedy, and the thick vegetable oil popular at the time, known as Colza oil and obtained from Cole or Rape seed, did not respond to capillary attraction sufficiently. To obviate this difficulty, the lamp was provided with a reservoir placed at a slightly higher level than the top of the wick, and the oil flowed to it by gravity. Normally, this resulted in a surplus which dripped into an overflow cup provided for the purpose. Typically of eighteenth-century design and craftsmanship, the Argand lamp shows the prevailing taste and quality of finish in the form of both reservoir and burner. The former often taking the shape of a Classical urn and the latter, although its outline was dictated by its function, was trimmed carefully with mouldings and with a pendant ornament at the base to match the finial at the top of the reservoir, The majority of these lamps were well-made and of brass, often finished with lacquer or, occasionally, with gilding.

Among the lamps that competed with the Argand for attention in America, but without equalling it in efficiency, was the *Agitable*. One of the attractions of this was that it could be sold cheaply, and after stressing this important point a New York importer advertised its other virtues as follows in 1795: 'The peculiar advantage of this invention is that it entirely removes the original objection to lamps, which was the great inconvenience of spilling oil; but it is curious in these, that in the most violent motion, held horizontal or even inverted, the oil cannot escape, and by their being made airtight the oil (like the quicksilver in a weather glass) is defended from the pressure of the atmosphere, which as well as preventing its coagulating, causes it

Figure 7. An 'Agitable' lamp.

to slip much lighter and further to the burners, burn brighter, and if properly trimmed with fresh cotton and fine oil, will not want snuffing while burning through twelve or fourteen hours continuance.' This fulsome 'puff' refers to a very simple type of lamp which comprises a reservoir with a burner holding one or more wicks fitted tightly in short tubes. The popularity of the Agitable was probably due to the fact that it burned whale-oil, which was plentiful in America. Variations of this lamp continued to be made for a further fifty years or so, and were described also as *Common* and *Patent* by different manufacturers.

The problem of feeding an adequate supply of oil to the Argand-type burner continued to be tackled during the remaining years of the century, and success was achieved finally in 1800. Then, B. G. Carcel devised a method incorporating a small clockwork pump. Having ensured that the oil was driven to where it was wanted, it was then necessary to control the quantity and prevent a surplus.

Franchot's 'Moderator' lamp, invented about 1836, achieved this, and rapidly gained favour.

The ultimate change was one of fuel, and with the discovery of the vast deposits of crude oil in Pennsylvania in 1859 came the paraffin lamp. With one or more wicks it gave a clean and clear light, did not smell unduly, and the fuel was drawn up the wick easily by capillary action without the need of clockwork or other devices. This meant that the reservoir could be in one piece with the burner, and the separate gravity-feed reservoir was no longer necessary.

Hanging lamps, consisting of a bowl of oil with a floating wick, suspended from the ceiling by three or more chains, were known in Roman times. In the seventeenth and eighteenth centuries the preference was for candle-burning chandeliers, but occasionally lamps were used. Robert Adam designed a number of them, and some of these remain in the houses for which they were made. In the early nineteenth century, others, made of bronze or bronze and ormolu like earlier examples, embody in their ornamentation the Greek, Egyptian and Gothic motifs which vied with one another at the time. These latter were fitted usually with Argand burners, and a central reservoir for the oil.

Lanterns. A few bronze hand lanterns from early times are preserved in museums, but they are rare survivors. The majority to be seen are no older than the seventeenth century, and most of them are much younger than that. Their main construction is of iron or brass, but the sheets of thin horn through which the candlelight shone dimly point to the reason for their old name: Lanthorn. Lanterns faced with glass often had it in the form of a bulging bull's-eye: with the glass swelling in the centre to form a simple lens and concentrate the light. Mica, imported from India, has also been used to protect the candle-flame: either because it is known geologically as Muscovite, or because the Russian Navy at one time used the materials for porthole windows, it was once known as Muscovy Glass. The hand lantern was a strictly utilitarian article, and was made and sold cheaply. Doubtless it was given rough treatment and cast aside when damaged; which explains why old examples are uncommon.

A more sophisticated form of lantern became popular in the eighteenth century: the Hall Lantern. It resembled its poor outdoor relation only in that the candle or candles it held were protected from draughts. While Thomas Chippendale showed designs for 'Lanthorns' in his *Director*, these were intended probably for making in wood, but specimens of similar design in gilt brass are known.

A very large lantern of gilt copper was once at Houghton Hall, Norfolk, and held no fewer than eighteen candles; its size caused much comment when it was installed in about 1720, and it was sold some years later. Of about the same date is 'a large glass Lanthorn with a wrought brass frame and a gold Crown to the top', which was made at a cost of £138 for use in Hampton Court Palace. It remains today where it was first hung, on the Queen's Great Staircase in the palace. Records show that this was an expensive one, but that others, no doubt smaller and simpler in design, could be bought for less money.

Robert Adam designed a number of lanterns for manufacture in gilt or brass, and some of these survive in the houses for which they were made. Typically, they show Classical features and are besprinkled with honeysuckle flowers, rams' heads and festoons of husks.

Both the Chippendale and Adam designs continued to be made long after the eighteenth century. A shortage of period examples has encouraged makers to produce them today, and to the inexperienced eye it is far from easy to know old from new.

Lecterns. The copper, brass or bronze lectern in the form of an eagle with outstretched wings is not uncommonly seen in churches throughout the world, but the reason for this association of an eagle with a book-support is not clear. It was the emblem of St John the Evangelist, which is appropriate for its connexion with books of the Gospels, and it has been suggested that as the desk often held psalm and hymn books it was a suitable choice, 'since as the eagle in its flight soared towards the sky, so the chanters' voices sought to reach the highest heavens'.

There are records of eagle lecterns dating back to the thirteenth century, and there is a drawing of one in one of the illuminations in the Luttrell Psalter, in the British Museum, written about the year 1300. A lectern bearing the date 1496 is in the church of St Gregory, Norwich, and there are others of the same period in churches up and down England. As with much ecclesiastical brasswork there is often a doubt as to where particular pieces were made: in the British Isles or on the mainland of Europe. Also, it must be remembered that designs have varied little during the past 650 years, and lecterns of similar pattern to those popular in the past are still being made.

Although the eagle was certainly the most popular subject for lecterns, other birds, and occasionally animals, were used. The lectern in Norwich Cathedral is in the form of a pelican, probably continental and of mid-fourteenth century date, but restored after it was recovered from being buried and hidden from Puritan iconoclasts in 1643.

Lighting appliances. Probably metals have played a larger part in the sphere of artificial lighting than they have in any other, and of the metals copper, either alone or in the form of an alloy, has had the major share. While pottery, porcelain and glass have all been used from time to time, it is metal that is the safest and most durable material for the purpose; it has been, and still is, the most widely used.

The devices used for lighting were limited by the medium employed, and these changed very little from prehistoric times until shortly after 1859; the year in which oil was found in Pennsylvania and a new fuel, paraffin or kerosene, became available cheaply and in enormous quantities. The simplest of all lights was obtained from a rush dipped in tallow, usually held in the grip of a rush-light holder made of iron, and therefore outside the scope of this volume.

Tallow is animal fat, melted and refined by straining to remove any impurities. An eighteenth century writer noted: 'A tallow candle to be good must be half sheep's, and half bullock's tallow; for hog's tallow makes the candle gutter, and always gives an offensive smell, with a thick black smoke. The wick ought to be pure, sufficiently dry, and properly twisted, otherwise the candle will emit an inconstant vibratory flame, which is both prejudicial to the eyes and insufficient for the distinct illumination of objects.' In some lands various trees and shrubs produce fruits containing tallow, and although some of it burns with a noticeably unpleasant smell it is cheap and convenient to use. Tallow, both animal and vegetable, was used for candle-making for many centuries, and about 1750 spermaceti, found inside the head of the huge sperm whale, was introduced in England for the same purpose. Alternatively, beeswax was used for making candles of the most reliable and more expensive types. John Evelyn wrote in 1654 that Doncaster, in Yorkshire, was 'famous for greate Wax-lights'.

Although tallow candles were comparatively cheap to buy they had the disadvantage of needing constant attention while burning. If not attended carefully the wick bent over as it burned, the candle 'guttered' and melted wax ran down the side; the result was smoke, smell and waste. The burning wick had to be cut to the correct length (snuffed) all the time it was in use, but since about 1820 candles have been made from stearine wax and have had plaited wicks which avoid this trouble and are consumed completely in the flame. On the other hand, the beeswax candle, if made correctly, will burn for a considerable length of time without any attention, and these were used almost always in churches and on social occasions in the better-class home.

The cost of candles varied, but there are references to their purchase in diaries and other old documents. Lord

Bristol noted in his diary that he bought eight dozen wax candles at 2s 4d a pound on 2nd February, 1739. A less wealthy country dweller, Henry Purefoy of Shalstone, Buckinghamshire, wrote to a chandler in a nearby town and said: 'I desire you would make me so many pounds of candles as you have had pounds of fat of me and make them the same size as the pattern.' Although it is not a difficult matter to make a candle, their manufacture was controlled strictly by the Tallowchandlers' and Waxchandlers' Companies. Both did their best to protect the interests of their members, and to regulate the quality of their productions. In return, Acts of Parliament were passed in their favour, and those caught transgressing were treated with severity; although it would seem, on occasion, with sympathy. A news item of 1769 recorded: 'A baronet was convicted by a bench of justices at Barnet, in the penalty of £3,100 for making his own candles; but the penalty was mitigated to £110 before the justices left the court.'

Additional protection was afforded to the Companies, and considerable revenue was raised for the use of the Exchequer, by taxes on candles. In 1710, this amounted to 4d a pound on wax candles, and a ½d a pound on those of tallow, but in the following year these figures were doubled. Rush-lights, 'only for private use, not sold nor made for sale, and but once dipped in grease and not in refined tallows', were allowed free of duty.

A candle is made from solidified grease, and its use was limited to those countries where the climate was not normally so hot as to melt the wax or tallow. The oil-lamp, using much the same substance in its liquid form as a basis, was popular in less temperate lands but used equally widely elsewhere. In the case of candle or oil-lamp the wick, whether of fabric or some other kind of vegetable matter, is an essential component.

Oils used for burning at different periods have varied with the locality and the available supply. Olive oil is mentioned in the Bible, where the Children of Israel were commanded to provide for the Ark of the Covenant 'pure olive oil beaten for the light to cause a lamp to burn continually'. The most popular in the eighteenth and early nineteenth centuries were Train oil and Colza oil, the former obtained by boiling the blubber of whales, and the latter, which was known also by the names of Rape oil and Carcel oil, made from the crushed seeds of certain types of kale. Almost any inflammable liquid was in use at one time or another in some part of the globe, and nearly all had in common the facts that they smelled whether burning or not and they were messy to handle.

A distillation of turpentine, known as Camphine oil, was employed widely between about 1830 and 1850, but being alarmingly prone to explode it fell into disfavour. *Paraffin oil*, known also as *Kerosene*, produced from petroleum, was a great advance on anything used before, and not long after it was first produced in quantity in America in about 1860 it was lighting the homes of tens of thousands of people. *See* **Candlesticks, Chandeliers, Lamps and Lanterns.**

Lock plates. The lock plate is a shaped ornament about the keyhole of a door, and incorporates a handle. Lock plates were introduced in England in the middle of the eighteenth century, when the ornamented box lock was displaced by the concealed mortice lock. The handle connects with the lock and bolt, and almost always the actual keyhole is hidden behind a moveable cover.

Earlier examples were of shaped outline and decorated with engraving. Those designed by Robert Adam were of more elaborate pattern, and their castings, finished with gilding, incorporated the classical motifs fashionable at the time.

Locks and Keys. Both the mechanism of the lock and the working part of the key were made usually of steel, but the case of a lock and the bow (or handle) of a key were often of brass. This was particularly common in England from the second half of the seventeenth century. Then, locks were screwed to one of the two sides of a door, and the visible brass case was engraved elaborately, and often overlaid with a pierced plate of the same metal. Similar pierced or cast overlays of brass were applied sometimes to lock-cases of blued steel.

The names of the Bickford family who probably worked in London, John Wilkes of Birmingham, and Richard Hewse of Wootton Bassett, Wiltshire, are associated with work of the highest quality, and examples are to be seen occasionally on the doors for which they were made. In 1688 Sir Richard Myddelton bought some locks for his home, Chirk Castle in Denbighshire, and the purchase was recorded by his steward as follows: 'Paid John Wilkes, of Birmicham, smith, for a brass lock and key with my master's coat of arms thereon £6, and for a brass lock and key for an escritoire £1.'

With the introduction in the middle of the eighteenth century of the mortice lock, which was let into the woodwork of the door and did not show when it was shut, decoration was applied no longer to the lock itself. Instead, it was employed on the lock plate: usually also of brass, and of which one was placed on either side of the door. Each lock plate was fitted with a handle connecting with the lock, and a hole, usually concealed by a moveable cover, through which the key could be used.

Brass-cased locks for cabinet work did not come into general use until the middle of the eighteenth century. They were made in many patterns, but were mostly entirely devoid of ornament and of simple construction.

The earlier cabinet locks were spring-loaded bolts in which the wards (raised pieces of metal that prevented the turning or correct placing of the wrong key) were the only obstacle. The tumbler lock which followed was slightly more complex, and in addition to the wards had a spring-loaded tumbler to be raised to a pre-determined height before the bolt could be moved. The well-known lever lock was introduced by Robert Barron in 1778, and substituted levers for the tumbler. Any reasonable number of levers could be fitted, but these had to be raised to exactly the correct height, and not higher, before the lock would operate.

In 1784, Joseph Bramah invented his patent lock, which was used extensively on much better-quality furniture from then onwards. It is recognized at once by the cylindrical brass projecting keyhole on the drawer- or door-front, and the name of the maker stamped on the case. The key is small and distinctive, being little more than a normal bow with a short tube having notches cut at the end.

Microscopes. *See* **Scientific instruments.**

Mirrors. The use of a plate of polished metal for the purpose of reflecting goes back far in the history of many countries, and was possibly one of the early uses of the material. Weight was a factor normally limiting the size to that of a hand-mirror, the shape was generally circular with a handle attached, and the appearance of an old example differs little from that of one to be found on a modern dressing-table. Both the back of the polished plate and the handle were treated with ornament which varied in style with the period of making. The early mirrors were of bronze, which retained a high polish and was slow to tarnish. Surviving examples have been excavated from tombs or recovered from where they were discarded centuries ago, but are now badly scarred in consequence of past neglect.

The Chinese are known to have made bronze mirrors at least as early as the Chou dynasty, which began in about 1122 B.C. They employed for the purpose an alloy containing a higher proportion of tin than usual in order to obtain a white metal. Many Chinese and Japanese mirrors are ornamented with designs in high relief on their backs, and it was found that when held so that they reflected sunlight on to a smooth surface they projected a disc of light together with a picture of the pattern on the back. The cause of this apparently magical effect remained a mystery for many centuries, but finally modern investigators examined the phenomena scientifically. They came to the conclusion that it was due to minute irregularities on the shiny surface, quite invisible to the eye, caused by pressure of the cast raised design on the reverse when polishing was in progress.

In the first century B.C. bronze mirrors were made in England, and some specimens with their backs and handles finely decorated have been excavated. Bronze, again, was used by the Romans, but they often faced the front surface with *speculum*, an alloy of copper and tin. This metal, known also as *steel*, was used in England long after the Romans had departed.

Steel or speculum may be seen occasionally, but is rare: most of it probably went into the melting-pot when glass supplanted metal for the purpose. In 1588 there was one at Leicester House, seat of the Earl of Leicester, described as 'in a verie faire frame, with beares and ragged staves (the crest of the Earl was a bear holding a ragged staff) on the top, with a steele glasse in it'. Metal mirrors continued to be made for scientific purposes; for use in microscopes, telescopes, etc.

Monumental brasses. These are the flat engraved bronze or brass plates used as memorials from the thirteenth to the seventeenth centuries. They are important because they often give a clear representation of clothing and armour and the changes that took place in them during the centuries, and they have been the subject of considerable study and many books. Together with illuminations in manuscripts they often form the only authority for the apparel of our ancestors.

The brasses were engraved on flat sheets of metal and, in the case of almost all English examples, the form of the person represented was cut out in outline. This conventionalized figure, or the entire rectangular plaque in most foreign brasses, was then laid down on a stone indented to receive it. Most of them were placed on the floors of churches where, unlike carved statues, they did not obstruct the space required for services.

It has been calculated that about 10,000 brasses remain in English churches, and many hundreds are to be found in the countries of the Continent. Each nation had its own artists at the craft, with national characteristics, but there was a certain amount of interchanging: Flemish brasses are to be seen in England, especially in East Anglia, and there are English brasses in several European countries.

Normal wear-and-tear, together with pillage, have reduced drastically the number of brasses remaining. France especially lost great quantities at the time of the Revolution, and of these, the only surviving evidence is a series of drawings in the British Museum. In England there was similar destruction at the time of the Reformation and later, but fortunately it was less extensive. John Evelyn visiting Lincoln in August 1654 noted in his Diary: 'The soldiers had lately knocked off most of the brasses from the gravestones, so as few inscriptions were left; they told us that these men went in with axes and hammers, and shut themselves in, till they had rent and torn off some barge-loads of metal, not sparing even the monuments of the dead, so hellish an avarice possessed them.'

In other countries the story is little different, but a remarkable assembly of brasses has luckily escaped the hand of destruction. Those include these of the Bishop of Werden in Germany; King Menved and his Queen, at Ringsted in Denmark; and Sir John D'Aubernoun, at Stoke D'Abernon, Surrey, in England. All of them dating from the thirteenth and fourteenth centuries.

The study of monumental brasses can be less arduous and involve less travel than may be imagined, for there are large collections of rubbings of them in London (Victoria and Albert Museum), and elsewhere. Rubbings are of the actual size of the originals, and are made by covering the brass with a sheet of paper which is then rubbed over with heel-ball: a soft black wax used by shoemakers for a very different purpose. It is suggested that readers who wish to make their own rubbings in a church should first ask permission to do so.

Mortars. These bowls of bell-metal were used, in conjunction with round-ended rods of the same metal called *pestles*, to reduce to powder both chemicals and cooking-ingredients. Generally, they went out of use in the nineteenth century when steam power enabled grinding to be done more cheaply and quickly on a large scale.

Metal mortars go back in date at least to the fourteenth century, but there is a lack of information about their making at all periods. It is agreed, however, that they were a by-product of bell manufacture; this is confirmed not only by the fact that they were made of bell-metal, but examples exist bearing the names of men who are known to have been bell-founders.

Mortars were made in most European and Asian countries and those of seventeenth-century Italy and Holland were exported in large numbers. The most interesting of them were moulded with bands of ornament, and with the name of the maker or his client and the year of manufacture in raised letters and numerals. Specimens measuring some fifteen inches in diameter and weighing as much as one hundredweight (112 lb.) have been recorded.

Late in the eighteenth century plain and undecorated mortars were made in England and elsewhere, and these are comparatively common. It should be mentioned that some of the old mortars, especially those of Dutch and Italian make, have been copied cleverly in recent years.

Musical instruments. Brass musical instruments, forerunners of those in use at the present time, date back many centuries, and in most instances have been improved beyond recognition both to eye and to ear, during the intervening years. Others were made of wood, but with reinforcements of brass. An example of the latter is the aptly-named *serpent*, a bass cornet of some eight feet in length. In order to make such an instrument practical to play and portable, the leather-covered tube of which it was constructed was coiled in a zigzag into a reasonable compass until it resembled its namesake in appearance. The holes by which it was played, in the manner of a recorder, were often bushed with ivory, but the tube leading to the mouthpiece and the outside of the open end emitting the sound were made of brass. It was succeeded by an instrument named the *ophicleide* (sometimes *serpentcleide*) made wholly of brass, and then by the *tuba*.

Turning to the percussion group; the humble tambourine was known to the Romans, and did not differ at all from the circular parchment-covered wood hoop with metal jingles familiar today. Cymbals, basin- or saucer-shaped brass discs that are crashed together or tapped with a stick, also were known centuries ago. In their day they have been treated with seriousness, for in 1705 a German writer published a lengthy book on these simple instruments and their use in earlier times, and followed it up twelve years later with another volume on the same subject. When they are called for in large orchestras the cymbals are played by a man who stands majestically to perform the task, but during the present century they have been mounted also on portable stands for operation by the foot of a drummer. In this manner their crashes, often somewhat muffled, make an accepted rhythmic background noise for dance and jazz music.

The coaching horn, several feet in length, has its slender tube made of copper and usually a silver or silver-plated mouthpiece. Sometimes they are still with the contemporary woven wicker or leather cases in which they were once strapped to the coach within reach of the guard. Small hunting horns are constructed in a similar manner. Both are to be found in antique shops, and both frequently pretend to be much older than they really are.

Ormolu mounts: 1. China. When porcelain was brought first to Europe from the Far East it was treated with the veneration it had merited from years of anticipation: its reputation had long preceded its arrival, along with many fables as to its mysterious origin and manufacture. The few articles reaching the West from the fourteenth century onwards were the perquisite of Royalty and the most wealthy nobles. Many of these pieces on their arrival were mounted carefully in silver or silver-gilt frameworks, in some instances inset with precious stones or enamelled in colours, and quite a few have survived intact to the present day. The mounts not only helped to preserve the china from damage, but they also enhanced its appearance in European eyes and, at the same time, the settings of precious materials stressed the regard in which these rarities were held by their owners.

In the first part of the eighteenth century the French began to make a speciality of mounting Chinese and other porcelain in ormolu: gilt bronze. This was done principally to heighten its decorative effect, and to enable it to blend with the extravagant rococo surroundings in which it was placed. At that time the fashion for Eastern works of art was at its height, but many of the imported articles were quickly Europeanized: lacquer panels, for instance, being cut up and made into pieces of furniture. All acted as inspirations to artists and designers, and the general effect of some of the fashionable rooms of the period was of fairy-tale Oriental abodes.

All types of porcelain were used for mounting, and frequently the porcelain flowers made successfully at Sèvres from about 1747 were added. These were affixed to the branches of ormolu or painted metal 'trees' sprouting from elaborately modelled bases, and framing figures or groups. Vases, bowls, cups, saucers; all were pressed into service with the proviso that the ultimate effect must be attractive. This often led to excesses in which, for example, pairs of bowls were mounted edge to edge without any regard to their painted pattern or to their possible usefulness.

Amongst the many talented, and mostly anonymous, artists who are thought to have designed mounts for porcelain are the following:

THOMAS GERMAIN; son of the goldsmith Pierre Germain, and famous himself in that craft. Some of his designs were published in 1748.

JEAN CLAUDE DUPLESSIS; born in Italy and originally bearing the surname Chiamberlano. About 1740 he came to Paris, and eventually designed porcelain for the Sèvres factory as well as metalwork of all kinds. His son, Jean Claude Thomas Duplessis, was also a sculptor and metalworker.

JUSTE AURELE MEISONNIER; born in Turin but worked principally in Paris. An important designer of metalwork, as well as a painter, sculptor and architect, he published a number of books of designs.

All these men, and many others, did not design any one type of metalwork, and it is usually difficult or impossible to be certain by whose hand any particular example was originally drawn. None of the existing pieces are signed, and most of the suggested identifications are based on a similarity rather than on a positive likeness.

In Germany, ormolu mounts were made also for porcelain but they are rarely up to the standard of the French work they strive to imitate. The quality of both design and finish is usually far below that of Paris.

English gilt-metal mounts on china are rare, but it is probable that the mounts found on some examples of Chelsea and Bow were made in the same country as the porcelain. Bow, indeed, is often to be identified by square holes in the backs of figures and groups, that would appear to have been made intentionally for holding metal arms for candle-holders. Mounts found on these pieces, dating between 1755 and 1760, are not of outstanding quality. Matthew Boulton of Soho, Birmingham, made ormolu from about 1765, and some of his work is found on Wedgwood ware. He pressed his friend Josiah Wedgwood to send him further supplies of vases for the purpose, but Wedgwood was able to sell all he could make and did not want to execute additional orders of this kind. At this, it seems, Boulton threatened to start a manufactory of his own for making vases, and it was rumoured that in 1769 he engaged Nicholas Sprimont, formerly owner of the recently defunct Chelsea factory in London, to supervise it for him. However, the project came to nothing in the end, and in the early 1780's Boulton ceased to make ormolu.

In a letter to his partner, Thomas Bentley, Josiah Wedgwood wrote from London in 1768 describing the current rage for French ormolu. It reads as follows:

> 'Mr Boulton tells me I should be surprised to know what a trade has lately been made out of vases at Paris. The artists have even come over to London, picked up all the old whimsical ugly things they could meet with, carried them to Paris, where they have mounted and ornamented them with metal, and sold them to the virtuousi of every nation, and particularly Milords D'Anglaise, for the greatest rarities, and if you remember we saw many such things at Lord Bolingbroke's, which he brought over with him from France. Of this sort I have seen two or three old China bowls, for want of better things, stuck rim to rim, which have had no bad effect, but looked whimsical and droll.'

A further type of metal mount appeared in France in the early nineteenth century. It was made cheaply of pieces of thin stamped gilt metal and wire, and sometimes is ornamented with small enamelled flowers. It is found on small articles, like pin-trays, ring-holders, etc., of fanciful design, which were made in quantity for the tourists flocking to Paris after the downfall of Napoleon. These souvenirs are sometimes called 'Palais Royal', from the shopping arcades in that one-time Royal palace where many were offered for sale.

The French continued to mount porcelain in ormolu in the nineteenth and twentieth centuries, following the styles of earlier periods and often imitating the signs of age. The study of ormolu-mounted china is a difficult one; for not only must the age of the metal be considered, but also that of the porcelain. The latter can usually only be examined by the parts of the surface remaining visible, and the tell-tale base is concealed by metal. A piece of ormolu coated liberally underneath with brown or black stain should be treated with suspicion, but there are no hard and fast rules to follow in determining genuineness. Experience is the only sure guide.

Ormolu mounts: 2. Furniture. Gilt copper or brass mounts seem to have been used first on furniture in the Orient, and pieces imported into Europe from the East in the late seventeenth century introduced the fashion into the Occident. In many instances, not only was the lacquered furniture itself imitated, but the mounts were also reproduced.

At about the same date, André Charles Boulle began to adapt the Italian styles of inlaying articles of furniture, and shortly perfected the manner with which his name remains associated to this day. Not only are pieces from his workshop, and the workshops of his imitators, veneered with inlays of metal, but metal with the addition of gilding is used to enhance the effect. The gilt metal (ormolu) is moulded skilfully into feet, table corners, handles, and other forms that are not only pleasing to the eye but practical; for the delicate inlay is highly vulnerable and the mounts serve an important purpose in protecting it where necessary.

In England, less extravagant use was made of metal in

connexion with furniture, and apart from instances in which copies of Oriental lacquerwork were made, the use of it was confined to small handles, escutcheons and, occasionally, ornamental hinges.

With the steady rise of rococo design in France the makers and designers of ormolu came into their own, and their importance was little less than that of the designers and makers of woodwork. The brothers Slodtz, the Caffieri family, Charles Cressent, and others took great pains to integrate the pattern of the metalwork with that of the veneered cabinet-work, and the result of their efforts was some of the most sumptuous furniture ever made.

Perhaps the most successful of any of these designers and craftsmen was the man who stamped his rare productions with the four letters 'B.V.R.B.'', and whose identity remained a perplexing mystery until recently. He has now been identified as a cabinet-maker of Dutch origin named Van Riesenburgh, but although it is satisfying to be able to accord him the credit for his work to his face (as it were) pieces bearing his stamp have long been recognized as pre-eminent in both design and finish.

The influence of French furniture on that of England resulted in the making of a number of pieces in the Louis XV manner, and for which the ormolu mounts were certainly designed especially. The name of the London cabinet-maker, John Cobb, is associated with this type of work; a piece which was assumed to have come from his workshop fetched the high price of $70,000 (about £25,000) in New York in 1960. However, on the whole the English buyer did not like gilt metal, and if he happened to do so usually obtained his furniture from Paris. When not using inlay, the English cabinet-maker relied on carved and gilded wood for effect, and only in exceptional instances did he closely ape his French rivals by using metal.

More noticeably, the cross-Channel influence affected the design of English handles and other ornaments. Thomas

Chippendale showed two pages of engravings of escutcheons and handles in the 1761 edition of his famous pattern-book, *The Gentleman and Cabinet-Maker's Director*. Most of them adapt the asymetrical elements of the rococo, and, when they have not been discarded at some past date, remain to enhance the carefully chosen wood to which they are attached.

In the Louis XVI period, the restraint of current designs lessened the exuberance of metalwork as much as everything else, but its use on furniture continued. If possible, although less in evidence, it was even more finely finished, and the work of Pierre Gouthière is justly famous for its high quality.

Ormolu mounts: 3. Marble and Stone. Marbles and similar materials were often treated similarly to porcelain in the eighteenth century and later. There was then a great interest in all kinds of natural curiosities: unusually-marked geological specimens, rare stones, and extraordinary freaks of many types were collected, and commented on in the press. Some of the more decorative examples were mounted in ormolu as vases, or other objects. While so many of the stones are today widely familiar, it must be remembered that two centuries ago the world was a very much larger and more mysterious place, it still had vast unexplored areas, and the natural resources as well as the scenery of those parts were a source of wonder and romance.

The red and green porphyry of Egypt were known in Roman times, and their decorative value was then fully exploited. Equally, in the eighteenth century both types were used for many purposes, and their natural beauty enhanced in mounts of ormolu. Other marbles and stones were used in the same manner, and these include jasper, lapis lazuli and malachite: the two latter seldom being employed in the solid but used like rare woods in the form of a thin veneer.

The name of Pierre Gouthière is linked closely with much work of this type. Born in 1732 in the provinces, he came to

Paris sometime before 1758 and in that year married the widow of his employer, a gilder and chaser named Cériset. As a result, he took over the latter's business, and before long was working for both Royal and noble clients. One of his patrons was the Duc d'Aumont, a member of the Court of Louis XVI, who bought 'two vases made from fragments of antique porphyry' in 1748, later obtained more rare marbles from Italy, and started a workshop in Paris for re-carving his purchases which were mounted by Gouthière. The catalogue of the auction sale of the collection formed by the Duc, held in 1782, contains a large number of ormolu-mounted pieces of all kinds, and those from Gouthière's workshop have the letter G added to their descriptions.

One of the finest pieces belonging formerly to the Duc d'Aumont is a perfume-burner, the body and the base made of red jasper, which was bought at the sale for Queen Marie Antoinette. Many years after the death of the Queen it was sold, and after several changes of ownership was bought in 1865 by the Marquess of Hertford. It is now in the Wallace Collection, London.

An English variety of fluorspar, named after the county in which it was found, Derbyshire Spar, is known also as Blue John: an anglicization of the French name for it, 'bleu-jaune', literally, blue-yellow. It is a vividly-marked blue, deep amethyst and yellow stone with transparent patches, that takes a high polish. It was mounted in ormolu both in France and England during the second half of the eighteenth century, and is found in the form of vases, candlesticks and candelabra. Matthew Boulton is credited with mounting pieces of the stone in England, and examples of work accredited to him are in the Victoria and Albert Museum, London, Windsor Castle, and elsewhere.

Pins. Pins made of bronze have survived from the Bronze Age, and have been made continuously since then of bronze or brass. The earliest specimens were doubtless used sparingly, and many of those excavated from ancient burial-grounds have decorative heads, which suggests that they had been used as much for ornament as for utility.

In more modern times, the French seem to have been suppliers of domestic pins in quantity to England from the fourteenth century. In that period the London Company of Pinners came into being, but opposition from abroad continued. In 1483, the first year of the reign of Richard III, Parliament prohibited pins 'to be imported by Strangers'; *i.e.* they might be brought into the country only by British subjects or established English dealers, and those no doubt to be members of the Company. Sixty years later, in 1543 under Henry VIII, a further Act was passed providing that 'no person shall put to sale any pinnes but only such as shall be double headed, and have the heads soldered fast to the shank of the pinnes, well smoothed, the shank well shaped, the points well and round filed, canted and sharpened'. This was enacted not only to ensure a good quality article being made, but to prevent traders from passing-off cheap iron pins which were treated to resemble those of brass and sold fraudulently at the higher price of the latter. Because it was either ineffective or unpopular, this law was soon repealed.

By 1626 a pin manufactory was started in Stroud, Gloucestershire, and flourished in spite of opposition from other makers who entered the trade in Bristol and Birmingham. They were all aided by Customs duties on imported pins levied during the seventeenth century, which amounted to a general duty of $7s$ $1d$ per dozen thousand, and the addition of $2s$ $4d$ per dozen thousand if of brass, or $4s$ $8d$ per hundredweight if of iron.

A writer of 1768 noted 'The London pointing and whitening are in most repute, because our pinmakers, in pointing, use two steel mills, the first of which forms the point, and the latter takes off all irregularities and renders it smooth, and as it were polished; and in whitening, they use block tin granulated: whereas in other countries they are said to use a mixture of tin, lead, and quicksilver; which not only whitens worse than the former, but is also dangerous, on account of the ill quality of that mixture, which renders a puncture with a pin thus whitened, somewhat difficult to be cured.' This may have been eighteenth century 'Buy British' propaganda, but the same writer adds words that apply today: 'The consumption of pins is incredible, and there is no commodity sold cheaper.'

Old brass pins were made in two parts: the body or shank from a length of wire which was cut and pointed, and the head from a couple of twists of thinner wire fitted tightly to the shank. Their manufacture was broken-down into stages, and eighteenth-century reports vary as to whether six or fifteen workers were employed on the various tasks between cutting the wire and sticking the finished pins into lengths of paper. Modern machine-made pins are in a single piece, and their heads are flat-topped when compared with those of their predecessors.

Pipes and Pipe-stoppers. Tobacco pipes were made sometimes of cast brass during the eighteenth century in England. Although undoubtedly more durable than clay, it is doubtful whether they gave as much satisfaction in use. Perhaps this accounts for the fact that they do not appear to have been made in quantity and are now rare. On the other hand, metal pipes of Japanese origin are not uncommon. Tobacco-smoking dates there from the seventeenth century, and while the wealthy used pipes of silver, the man-in-the-street could afford no better than brass.

Pipe-stoppers for pressing down the burning leaf in the bowl, were made of many materials including brass. An inch or two in height at the most, their design took many forms ranging from the severely functional to representations of hands and legs. While a few surviving specimens date from some time in the eighteenth century, the majority are later in date.

Powder flasks. Flasks for holding gunpowder were made in Germany as early as the sixteenth century. Specimens of gilt bronze are ornamented appropriately with sporting designs in relief, but surviving examples of this date are rare. More common, are later eighteenth/early nineteenth-century copper and brass flasks made in England. These are

Figure 8.

usually pear-shaped, and embossed with designs that vary from plain ribbing to elaborate arabesques.

Saucepans. *See* **Skillets.**

Scientific instruments. Copper and brass were, and still are, used extensively in the making of scientific intruments of all types. The Armillary Sphere, which is a celestial globe in skeleton form centring either on the Earth or the Sun, was known to the ancient Greeks and the Chinese. At the observatory in Pekin, built in the thirteenth century by the Mongol emperor Kublai Khan, is the great bronze Armillary made in 1279 by the celebrated astronomer of his day, Kuo Shou-Ching.

Tycho Brahe, the sixteenth-century Danish astronomer, developed the Armillary Sphere from the comparatively simple form in which it had remained since the time of Ptolemy. The related Astrolabe, introduced into Europe probably by the Arabs, took two forms: one for astronomy, and the other for marine use. It was the latter type that was of importance to navigators until the invention of the Sextant replaced it, and it was the Marine Astrolabe that aided Columbus on his voyage to America.

Marine instruments of brass were numerous, but the most important was the Sextant for determining the latitude of a ship at sea. This was devised almost simultaneously, and independently, by an Englishman, John Hadley, and an American, Thomas Godfrey of Philadelphia, about 1730.

The microscope and the telescope are among the many other instruments indebted to copper and its alloys for their construction in a practical form. The scientific and mechanical geniuses of all lands contributed over the years to the development of such instruments; some of them out-moded completely by later superior inventions, but others have changed little during the last 100 years and are still in use.

The water-clock, or Clepsydra, used by the ancient Egyptians, was made usually from brass or bronze. A simple type found in southern India comprised a copper bowl with a very small hole in the bottom; this was floated in a larger-sized container of water, and when the small basin had filled and sunk an attendant struck a gong to mark the passing of the period of time. Of more complicated pattern was one given to the Emperor Charlemagne by the King of Persia in the year A.D. 807. This is described as follows: 'The dial was composed of twelve small doors, which represented the hours; each door opened at the hour it was intended to represent, and out of it came the same number of balls, which fell one by one, at equal intervals of time, on a brass drum. It might be told by the eye what hour it was by the number of doors that were open, and by the ear by the number of balls that fell. When it was twelve o'clock twelve horsemen in miniature issued forth at the same time and shut all the doors.'

In the seventeenth century there was a revival of interest shown in the Clepsydra, and Sir Isaac Newton is said to have made one when a child. There are today far more allegedly genuine survivors than were ever made at the time, and potential buyers should carefully examine available specimens with this fact in mind.

The seventeenth century saw also the invention of the pendulum, and its application to the movement of a clock by Christiaan Huygens, the Dutch astronomer and mathematician, in 1656. There followed a rapid progress in clockmaking, which had been hitherto principally the province of iron-workers, and limited in the main to timepieces on public buildings. Only rarely was a portable clock, or one for use inside a house, attempted and results were not encouraging. Now that a reliable mechanism had been devised there was a wide demand to be filled. A new craft came into being: not only did the clockmaker cut the necessary gear wheels, drill front and back plates and shape innumerable small parts, but he also engraved dials and cast the decorative spandrels (corner-pieces) to go on them, and all were made of brass. In the course of the eighteenth century these different processes became individual trades, and the clockmaker often did little more than assemble the parts, test the finished product and then add his name on the face.

The earlier indoor wall-clocks were of open-sided construction with metal frames and turned columns at the four corners, and table-clocks had gilt brass or copper cases. In England these developed into the well-known lantern clock, with a bell on the top and brass doors at the sides to protect the moving parts from dust. The Lantern continued to be made until about 1730, but the wood-cased clock, which had been growing in popularity since 1670, finally won the day.

In France, metal played a larger part, for all during the eighteenth century (and also during the nineteenth), clocks were put into cases made of ormolu on which all the skills of designers and craftsmen were lavished. About 1780 there was a fashion in England for clocks in cases of this material, and in many instances they were mounted with figures and groups of unglazed white Derby porcelain. The name of the Royal clockmaker, Justin Vulliamy of London, is usually associated with them.

In spite of the many improvements that took place in both clock and watch mechanisms, the average examples were seldom as accurate as could be desired. Also, both were expensive and their ownership limited to the wealthier people. If a man wanted a rough indication of the hour at little cost he would continue to have recourse to the sun, and carry or consult an instrument that would tell him when it was at its highest altitude, or whether it was below or beyond the meridian.

The Sundial has been known for many centuries, and a mention of one in the Bible (Isaiah xxxviii, 8) dates from about 700 B.C. Apart from fixed examples, which remain in use today on churches and other buildings and in gardens, portable ones of pocket size were made in the past, and many of both types were of brass. The simplest of these small-sized instruments is the Ring-dial: a circular device which is held so that the sun can shine through a hole in the circumference. The ray of light falls on to the inside of the ring where a numeral is engraved corresponding to the hour. Another type resembles the outdoor Sundial, but is of small size and fitted with a compass and folding gnomon: the latter is the raised arm which throws the shadow, and is adjustable according to the latitude where it is being used. These small dials were very popular in all countries especially about 1700, and many of the surviving specimens still retain their shagreen-covered protective cases.

One of the best-known makers of pocket dials was an Englishman, Michael Butterfield, who worked in Paris. In the words of a contemporary, he was 'a very excellent artist in making all sorts of mathematical instruments, and works for the King (Louis XIV) and all the Princes of the Blood, and his work is sought after by all the nations of Europe and Asia'. Like the clockmaker, Thomas Tompion, Butterfield's fame was sufficiently great during his lifetime to encourage copyists, and these fakes together with others of later date outnumber the genuine works of both craftsmen.

Sextants. *See* **Scientific instruments.**

Skillets and Saucepans. The skillet is the forerunner of the saucepan. Both were made of bronze or bell-metal, but the former utensil is distinguished from the latter by having three short legs attached to the underneath. The purpose of the legs was to raise the pan above the embers when it was in use on a cottage 'down hearth'; a plain flat hearth without a grate, in which wood was the fuel.

A Roman skillet in the British Museum is shaped in the body like a cauldron (bellied at the sides, and with a rounded base), and has a flat handle ornamented with patterns in relief and in niello. It is inscribed with the name of the maker, Boduogenus, but it is suggested that its comparatively elaborate design indicates that it was used for sacrificial purposes.

The cauldron-bodied skillet, or Posnet, was made continuously until at least the fifteenth century, when it began to be replaced by one having a bowl with inward-sloping sides, a flat narrow rim at the wide top, and a flat base. By the seventeenth century it was usual to mould on the handle the name of the maker, or even a moral reflection. An example of the latter that would seem to have been popular is the grim reminder 'YE WAGES OF SIN IS DEATH', and among the names of makers are those of several men who were bellfounders.

In the eighteenth century came the introduction of copper cooking vessels. The earlier examples were made with rounded sides, while those of the nineteenth century are quite straight. A complete and shining *batterie-de-cuisine*, each single piece stamped or engraved with the original owner's crest or initials, is a splendid sight, and a great amount of labour must have been expended in a big kitchen in keeping it polished brightly.

All copper vessels were lined with tin as a precaution against poison released from the copper by acids in the contents, and there was considerable concern on the subject. A London newspaper paragraph of 1753 from Sweden, reads: 'A dissertation written at Paris is translated into our language by the approbation of the college of physicians; to make the public sensible of the danger of dressing victuals in copper and brass kettles, saucepans, etc., unless well tinned.' The Swedish Government shortly banned the making of all copper vessels for cooking, but in other countries, in spite of much debate on the subject, nothing further was done officially.

In England, in 1756 the Society of Arts pronounced on the matter and pointed out the dangers of tinning the insides of copper vessels with impure tin alloys. The Society said: "Tis therefore presumed, that for the future, none who value the health of their families, will use copper vessels untinned, or permit their pots, saucepans or other kitchen vessels to be tinned with a mixture of lead, in the former unwholesome manner. For lead is soon dissolved by vinegar, or even a weaker acid, and is known to be a slow poison; whereas pure tin is a harmless metal, not so easily dissolved, will last a great deal longer, and is little more expensive.' No doubt this and other publicity was effective, for adequately tinned copper utensils are still employed for cooking, and many people will use no others for the purpose.

Skimmers. These are flat-bowled spoonlike implements for skimming liquids: for removing cream from milk, fat from gravy, and so forth. Many examples were made of brass from at least the eighteenth century, and most have a slightly concave bowl four or five inches in diameter riveted to a brass or an iron handle. A similar article, known as a *Flit*, has the same type of bowl but the handle is in the form of a ring affixed to one side. These were used expressly for skimming milk, and must have been handy in dealing with the large wide-topped milk pans once commonly to be found in dairies.

Shoe horns. Johnson's Dictionary notes that this is 'A horn used to facilitate the admission of the foot into a narrow shoe'. It was made, as its name proclaims, of horn; in fact, they are still made of it with success in spite of attempts to rival the traditional material with modern plastics. Late in the eighteenth century (and later still) they were made from brass, often with elaborately curled handles which have the advantage of giving a good grip.

Snuffers. *See* **Douters.**

Spirit measures. *See* **Ale measures.**

Spoons. Spoons were made of brass in England in the sixteenth century. They were unpopular with makers of pewter and the Court of the Pewterers' Company in London agreed on 23rd September, 1567, that 'there should be no spoons made of brass or latten or any yellow metal, upon pain that if any person hereafter be found that he does make any such spoons shall forfeit and pay for every spoon 3/4d. The said spoons were lately invented by John God, and he has confessed he has made but three dozen, one dozen he has sold to one in Aldgate, and another stranger has bought one other dozen. And the third dozen the good man of the Castle (a tavern) in Wood Street must have them. And if there be found any more of the same God's making, he shall pay for every spoon 3/4d.'

This, and further orders of the same nature may explain why brass spoons of the period are extremely scarce. In the following century, many were made and there are a fair number of survivors. These spoons are of a similar shape to silver or pewter spoons of the same date: the bowl pear-shaped or rounded, and the thin handle terminating usually in a small ornamented knob. Varieties of handle are flat or hexagonal, and the tops include the following:

Cone: somewhat resembling a fir-cone
Acorn: as the fruit of the oak
Diamond-point: with a diamond-shaped terminal

Seated lion
Wrythen: a ball engraved with spiral cuts
Apostle: a standing figure of one of the apostles
Seal: a circular round-topped terminal.

A further type is known as 'Slipped in the stalk', and has the top of the handle cut off at an angle.

Later in the seventeenth century, the bowl of the spoon became elongated in shape and began to resemble modern ones. The top of the handle again took various forms, but the most popular was the one known variously as *Trefoil*, *Pied-de-biche* (Goat-foot) or *Split-end*: rounded, with two notches cut in it. A further development was the plain rounded end, which became fashionable during the reign of Queen Anne (1702–14), and is still a standard pattern.

Most latten spoons were marked in a manner similar to those of pewter or silver, but little is known of their makers. Some of the later spoons of brass were tinned, *i.e.* coated with molten tin to give them a silvery appearance, and some of these are stamped 'Double Whited'. In the course of time many thousands of old brass spoons must have been discarded. They were quite cheap to buy, did not stand up to continual wear, and a large proportion of the surviving specimens have been excavated from where they were lost or thrown away.

Sundials. *See* **Scientific instruments.**

Telescopes. *See* **Scientific instruments.**

Tobacco boxes. Tobacco boxes of metal were used in the eighteenth century for holding tobacco carried in the pocket, in the same way as a leather, rubber, or plastic pouch is used now. They were made of both copper and brass and in many countries, especially Holland and Germany. From the large number to be found in England, the Dutch in particular must have exported them in quantity.

The old Dutch boxes are usually oval in shape, with the hinged lid and the bottom engraved with pictures and words. The latter are often simple rhymes, but usually with a characteristic leaning to the facetious.

At Iserlohn, near Dortmund in Germany, was made a series of oblong boxes with rounded ends, embossed in relief with battle scenes. They are to be found in either copper or brass, and date from about 1760.

Eighteenth-century boxes of English make are usually of plain design, and engraved with a crest or coat-of-arms. Alternatively, they bear the name of the original owner. James Watt in his *Memoir* of Matthew Boulton, the Birmingham manufacturer, records the following: 'That company [meaning the East India Company] also wanted a large quantity of a peculiar sort of Tobacco boxes which Mr. Boulton contracted for at a very low price; which he was enabled to do by making them of Bath metal, which admitted of being struck when hot in very handsome forms; they could not have been made of brass at twice the money.'

Trivets. These are metal stands for holding a kettle, food, etc., to be kept hot before a fire. Most examples date from the

Figure 9. A brass-topped Trivet to stand in the grate or hook on a fire-bar.

eighteenth century and later, but rare survivors of earlier date are known. One in the Victoria and Albert Museum, London, is engraved with the date 1668.

Many are of iron, but brass ones were made perhaps for use in the parlour or sitting-room where their appearance was a matter of concern.

Trivets were made with three or four legs to stand on their own in the fireplace, and there were also legless types to hook on to the firebars or the fender. Many have bases or frames of iron, with pierced and moulded top plates of brass and turned wood handles. *See also* **Footman.**

Warming pans. As a human being grows older one of the less pleasant aspects of retiring to bed in the autumn and winter months is that of entering between icy-cold sheets, and doubtless this has been a common feeling for many centuries. It is said that regal and noble beds in medieval times were warmed by pages who lay in them naked until their masters saw fit to retire. Equally, the tradesman is alleged to have selected a suitably hot-blooded apprentice for the unenviable task.

Brass-bodied warming pans with long handles were made in Holland and England in the sixteenth century and onwards, and copper ones date probably from about the same time. In 1656 the Rev. Giles More recorded in his journal the purchase of one from a brasier in London named Johnson, 'at his shop in Grace Church Street', for the sum of 7s 6d. The earlier examples were made with iron handles, and it is said that those with brass ornament or rings at the upper ends are of continental origin. Later ones of all makes had wooden handles, often with an ebonized finish.

The lids of many of the better examples were elaborately pierced and engraved, and some have on them the coat-of-arms or initials of their original owner as well as the date when they were made or bought.

The warming pan was filled with glowing pieces of charcoal, and holes in the hinged cover allowed air to enter and keep the embers alive at the same time as the heat rose. Careless handling doubtless led to occasional fires, and fumes from the charcoal would eventually soil the bedclothes. A solution to these two difficulties was the nineteenth-century introduction of a warming pan with a round copper body of flattened elliptical shape, and with a screw-capped filling hole for hot water. They are claimed to be of Scottish manufacture. The long handle that had made the warming-pan a useful and picturesque household article for about three centuries disappeared, and the plain copper or earthenware bottle, still to be bought occasionally, took its place.

In America, John Halden, 'Brasier from London', advertised in 1744 that 'he makes and sells all sorts of copper and brass kettles, . . . warming pans', but it is not clear whether these were of his own manufacture or, as is probable, imported. The only American worker whose products in this category have been identified positively is Charles Hunneman of Boston. A few American-made warming pans of eighteenth-century date have been preserved, and although some bear the initials of their manufacturers these have not yet been identified.

Wax-jacks. In the late seventeenth and early eighteenth centuries Wax-jacks were used widely, and some of them were made of brass. They hold a length of tallow-covered wick which is unrolled as it is needed, and fed through a spring-loaded grip for burning. Their use was for melting wax for the sealing of letters long before the ready-gummed envelope was invented. Early settlers in America had a rather similar device which they called a 'Pull-up'.

Weights and Measures. The national standards for weights and measures were often made of brass or bronze; these being the most durable materials for the purpose.

In 1495 in the reign of Henry VII weights and measures were delivered at the Royal expense 'to all members of Parliament, knights of the shire, barons of the Cinque Ports, as burgesses of borough towns, to be deposited in all cities, towns corporate, and other convenient boroughs and towns having a constable, throughout their several districts, there to be and remain for ever as standards'.

It was then laid down by Act of Parliament that 'the measure of a bushel shall contain 8 gallons of wheat, and that every gallon shall contain 8 lbs. of wheat of Troy weight, and every pound contain 12 ounces of Troy weight, and every ounce contain 20 sterlings (penny-weights: dwts.), and every sterling be of the weight of 32 corns of wheat (grains) that grow in the midst of the ear of wheat, according to the old law of this land'.

Some of these very old standards have survived, but most were destroyed when new ones replaced them in later years. In the eighteenth century a further Act caused the making of a new set of standards. Most of the London set were lost or damaged when fire destroyed the Houses of Parliament in 1824, but some seventy years later the yard measure was rediscovered.

The constant remaking of weights and measures over the centuries was due to miscalculations on the part of makers, to changes in the sizes and shapes of the standards themselves caused by age and atmosphere, and to alternations in the systems of measurement. At one time there were no fewer than four legal bushel measures: for beer, wine, coal and corn, and it varied between eight and twelve gallons in capacity in different parts of the country.

In 1688, it was found that the standard wine gallon, kept at the Guildhall, London, had a capacity of 224 cubic inches, and that the ale quart at the Exchequer held $70\frac{1}{2}$ cubic inches. This latter would give a gallon (at four quarts to the gallon) of 282 cubic inches, but ignoring these discrepancies it was decided that the assumed measure of 231 cubic inches (the legal standard) should continue in use.

Bronze weights and measures were almost always engraved or moulded with the name or arms of the monarch in whose reign they were made, the year of manufacture and, sometimes, with the name of the city, town or county to which they belonged. *See also* **Ale and Spirit measures,** *and* **Wool weights.**

Wool weights. The most important product of England for many centuries was wool. As early as the reign of Edward III

(1327–77), in order to encourage weaving and allied industries foreign labour was imported, and the exportation of wool prohibited on pain of death; a prohibition that could be evaded if enough money was forthcoming to purchase a licence from the Crown. At the same time, it is said that the Woolsack, a large-sized cushion covered in red cloth, was placed as a seat for the Lord Chancellor in the House of Lords as a reminder of the importance of wool in the life of the nation. It may be added that the Woolsack, in spite of its attribution to an earlier king, is not mentioned in legislative documents before the time of Henry VIII.

The laws were changed often, and in the reign of Elizabeth I the trade was freed from many of the burdensome restrictions and flourished for some years. Under Charles II export was again forbidden, and the position remained unchanged, in law if not in the letter, until 1825. As a result, production overran demand, smuggling became rife, and artificial stimulants to increase consumption were put forward. One of these was a decree that all dead persons must be buried wearing a shroud made of wool.

In view of its importance it is not surprising that wool should have attracted taxation, and for this purpose the bundles of raw material were weighed. Special weights were decreed by the government for the purpose of checking the king's scales, which were set up at certain specified Staple towns and where all wool in a surrounding district had to be taken.

The weights were shield-shaped and made of bronze, and bore the Royal arms and the initials of the monarch incised or in relief. At the top of each weight is found a hole, stated to be for joining two of them together with a rope or leather strap for transport on horseback, but equally useful for suspending them from a beam scale. Wool was reckoned by the Tod, equivalent to 28 lb., and wool weights are found in divisions of this: 7 lb. and 14 lb. At the back of each weight there is almost always a circular depression which was made when removing surplus weight in testing against the standard. Elsewhere, there are one or more impressed marks, not unlike the hall-marks on silver, put there by the Founders' Company and the authorities at the Guildhall, in London. A further mark sometimes indicates the city, town or district in which the weight was used.

Wool weights were changed with each succeeding monarch, and it was forbidden for obsolete ones to be used. Some 100 to 150 old examples have been preserved, but it must be stressed that they have been forged widely during the past century.

APPENDIX A

Fakes

To differentiate between old and new in metal wares is no easier to do than to explain, but some general points may be of help to the reader. The most obvious differences to look for are signs of the cheaper manufacturing processes used for reproductions and, above all, the poor finish given to modern pieces compared with old. As an example, articles made originally by the *cire perdue* process are copied in moulds; the moulds are made to take apart for the removal of each casting, and where they join together they leave a raised line on the piece. Unless this is removed with skill there are bound to be traces of it visible to the keen eye. Frequently too much metal is ground away from such a join, and instead of a curved surface it will have been filed flat.

Again, simple articles like horse-brasses can be reproduced in sand moulds, but the sand may be of a coarse variety and both front and back of the brass will be heavily granulated in appearance. In the past, this was filed away carefully until no trace of the roughness remained, but that is an expensive business today. Instead, the piece is held against a fast-revolving grinder, usually only on the front, and not only is the granulation rubbed away but the whole thing is given a false air of being well worn. However, any parts below the upper level surface are untouched, and where there are pierced places these stay clogged and unsightly.

Bronzes lend themselves to forging in poor metals, such as spelter: a cheap alloy of which zinc is the principal ingredient. Daubed with stain, this makes a passable imitation of the real thing but, again, comparison will quickly prove a number of differences which will be obvious on future occasions.

APPENDIX A

Good Italian Renaissance bronzes are so rare that specimens must be viewed with suspicion unless their provenance is known. Although the love of a bargain is universal, a display of caution is called for when confronted with an object worth at least £1,000 which is priced at 7s 6d.

Brass candlesticks are copied frequently, and good copies of unusual types can be deceptive. Once more it is a question of fineness of finish, and an inspection of the underside of a genuine example will show that the care taken in smoothing and tidying the base and hidden parts is not to be found in present-day specimens. It is a question of giving the proven genuine article a careful and thorough study, and of comparing a doubtful piece with an accepted one so that the variations are understood thoroughly.

Eastern brassware inlaid with silver and copper has been made to the same, or similar, designs for some six or seven centuries, but as time has advanced the quality of design and workmanship has deteriorated. The precision with which genuinely early examples were made immediately shows up the clumsiness of more modern pieces, and the collector will soon find that the majority of available specimens are of nineteenth- or twentieth-century manufacture.

One of the most difficult kinds of metal in which to differentiate between old and new is French ormolu. The French continued their tradition of fine workmanship for a long time after the end of the eighteenth century, and Victorian (and later) copies of Louis XV and XVI pieces are not uncommon and are often very well done. In these instances, the later examples will be found to have been finished almost up to the standard of the originals, and considerable experience is usually needed before they can be told apart.

Mounts on porcelain are sometimes a little easier to date, although they, too, were made long after 1800 and in old styles of design. Usually they are found to have been

APPENDIX A

constructed in parts and, if so, the screws and nuts holding them together can provide a useful clue. Old nuts, in particular, are very roughly shaped, showing none of the machined precision of the modern square or hexagon, and the screw threads are often coarse. It must be remembered that these details are the easiest of all to fake, and the presence of old screws and nuts cannot be taken alone as evidence of genuineness.

APPENDIX B

Cleaning

IN connexion with ormolu it must be emphasized that it should never be cleaned with metal-polish of any kind. Undoubtedly great quantities have had the gilding removed by the over-zealous, and once the gilding has gone replacement is costly and not always satisfactory. If ormolu should need to be cleaned it can be washed with a weak solution of ammonia and water, but to do this all the separate parts must be unscrewed and each must be rinsed in clean water and dried thoroughly before re-assembly. When taking a piece apart it is as well to keep each nut with the screw on which it was found, as they are often not interchangeable.

Cleaning other types of metal is usually a specialized job, and the amateur can possibly do more harm than good. Much helpful information on the subject, and an idea of the complexities, will be found in a book entitled *The Conservation of Antiquities and Works of Art*, by Dr H. J. Plenderleith, published in 1956.

INDEX

ADAM, Robert, 111, 112, 116
Africa, 29
Agitable, 109–10, fig. 7
Agricola (George Bauer), 14
Aich's metal, 23
Alchemists, 13
Ale and Spirit measures, 59–60, fig. 3
Ale warmers, 60
Alms dishes, 60
America, 29–30, 71–72
Andirons, 30, 60–62, 92
Antimony, 16, 23
Aquamaniles, 31, 62–63, 91–92
'Arabesque' ornament, 49
Argand, Ami, 108
Argand oil-lamp, 76, 108–9, 110, 111
Argentan, 22, 44
Armillary Sphere, 132
Arsenic, 16
Ashanti, 29
Ashtadhatu, 27
Assyrians, 28
Astrolabe, 132–3
Augsburg, 38
Aumont, Duc d', 129

'B.V.R.B.', 127
Baghdad, 48
Baillie, Lady Grissell, 83
Barron, Robert, 118
Bath metal, 26, 68, 140
Battering, 17
Battersea, 20
Bauer, Georg (Agricola), 14
Bede, 64–65
Bedsteads, 63–64
Beeswax candles, 114
Belgium, 30–31, 45
Bell, William, 70
Bell metal, 22, 64, 73, 121, 136

Bells, 45, 64–65, 92
Benin bronzes, 29
Bernward, Bishop of Hildesheim, 38
Bidri work, 47
Bihar, 47
Bini, 29
Birmingham, 42, 68
Blue John, 24, 129
Boduogenus, 136
Bologna, Giovanni, 50
Bolsover, Thomas, 44
Boston, 30
Boulle, André-Charles, 81, 102–3, 126
Boulton, Matthew, 24, 25, 42, 43, 44, 68, 76, 108, 125, 129, 140
Brahe, Tycho, 132
Bramah, Joseph, 118
'Branch', 78, 81
Brass, 22; *see also under object required*
Braziers, 65–66
Brighton, Royal Pavilion, 82
Briosco, Andrea, 50
Bristol, Lord, 115
Britannia metal, 22–23
British Museum, 29, 39, 66, 92
Bronze, 21–22; *see also under object required*
Bronze Age, 17, 39, 66, 96, 129
Bronze dorée, 24
Bronzes, African, 29
  Chinese, 33–36
  faked, 146–7
  German, 38
  Indian, 46–47
  Islamic, 50
  Italian, 49–50, 147
  Japanese, 50–51
  Luristan, 48
Buckets, 66–67

INDEX

Buckingham Palace, 82
Buddhism, 46
Burgos, 55
Burma, 32
Butterfield, Michael, 135–6
Buttons, Button-making, 18–19, 67–72
Byers, James, 30
Byzantium, 49

CADIZ, 28
Caffeiri family, 24, 81, 127
Cairo, 48, 49
Calamine, 16–17, 30
Cambacères, 88–89
Cambodia, 47
Camphine oil, 116
Candelabra, 77–78, 129
Candleholders, folding, 77
Candles, 114–5
Candlesticks, 30, 31, 38, 41–42, 45, 54, 55, 72–77, 129, 147
Canton enamel, 19, 36–37
Carcel, B. G., 110
Carlton, House, 25
Cauldrons, 39, 66–67
Celtic art, 28–29
Censers, 78
Cériset, 129
Ceylon, 47
Champlevé, 19
Chandeliers, 78–83
Ch'e-Chin, 32
Chenets, 62
Chestnut roasters, 83
Chiamberlano, 124
Ch'ien Lung, 37
Chills, 106, fig. 6
Ch'in, 35
China, 25, 28, 31–37, 47, 118
China-stone, 19
Ching-t'ai, 36
Chippendale, Thomas, 91, 112, 128
Chou, 32, 35, 118

Chung, 34
Chuo, 34
Cire perdue, 17–18, 29, 33, 46, 53, 63, 73, 146
Clepsydra, *see* Water-clocks
Clocks, Clockmaking, 134–5
Cloisonné, 19–20, 36, 53–54
Coaching horns, 122
Coal scuttles, 83–84, fig. 4
Cobb, John, 127
Collins metal, 23
Colza oil, 109, 116
Company of Mines Royal, 41
Coral, 47
Cornwall, 15, 16, 28, 43
Cornwell and Martin, 71–72
Corona, 79
Cots, 63
Crassets, 106
Cressent, Charles, 127
Crete, 28
Crusies, 106–7
Cups, 39
Curfews, 84–85
Curtain-holders, 85
Cymbals, 122
Cyprus, 13

DAMASCENING, 19, 47
Damascus, 19, 48, 49
De re metallica, 14
Delta metal, 23
Denmark, 42
Derbyshire Spar, *see* Blue John
Dinanderie, 31
Dinant, 30–31, 45, 74
'Donkey's ear', 60
Door knockers, 85–87
Doors, 49
Douters, 87–88, 107
Dover, 97
Duplessis, Jean Claude, 124
Duplessis, Jean Claude Thomas, 124

INDEX

Durham Cathedral, 73, 79
Durham, County, 39, 66
Dutch foil, 23
Dutch metal, 23

EDICT OF NANTES, revocation, 41
Egypt, 28, 48, 55
Electro-plating, 22, 44
Enamelling, 19–20, 21, 36, 97
Engravers' plates, 89–90
Escutcheons, 90–91
Evelyn, John, 81, 114, 120
Ewers, 56, 91–92
Extinguishers, 77, 88

FAKES, 35, 50, 146–8
Falun, 55
Famille rose, 37
Famille verte, 33
Fawley Court, 93
Fenders, 92–94
Fire-dogs, 60–62
Fire-irons, 94
Flanders, 77
Flit, 137
Flyer, 98
Footman, 94
Forks, 94–95
Frames, 95
France, 37–38, 40, 78
Franchot's 'Moderator' lamp, 111
Fujiyama, 52

GANESHA, 46
George IV, 82
Germain, Thomas, 124
German silver, 22, 44
Germany, 16, 38–39, 40, 41, 45, 56, 60, 139
Ghana, 29
Gido, 53
Gilding, 19, 47, 50, 91, 109

Gilt brass, 85, 90, 91
Gilt bronze, *see* Ormulu
Gloucester Candlestick, 72–73
Godfrey, Thomas, 133
Gold, 19, 26, 27, 34, 47, 52
Gold leaf, 23
Gongs, 95–96
Gothic, 44–45
Gouthière, 128–9
Granada, 48
Grates, 92–94
Graye, Miles, 64
Greasepans, 74, 75, 79
Great Britain, 14, 15, 39–45
Gun metal, 23

HADLEY, John, 133
Halden, John, 30, 142
Hamadan, 48
Hames, 98
Hampton Court Palace, 112
Hanukkah lamp, 73–74
Harz, 30, 38
Heath, George, 104–5
Heath, William, 104
Helsbury Quarry, 39
Hervey, John, 26
Hewse, Richard, 117
Hold-back, 85
Holland, 41, 42, 45–46, 80, 139
Horns, 96–97
Horse brasses, 97–102, 146, fig. 5
Houghton Hall, 112
Hsüan Ho Po Ku T'ou Lu, 33
Hu, 34
Huai, 35
Hungary, 13
Hunneman, Charles, 30, 141
Huygens, Christiaan, 134

IFE, 29
Ikons, 54
India, 46–48
Ink-inlaying, 52

Inlaying, 19, 34, 47, 48, 52, 56, 68, 102–3, 127
Iran, 48
Iraq, 48, 49
Iron, 13, 16, 23, 27, 61, 66, 78, 93, 141
Iserlohn, 39, 140
Islam, 48–49, 56, 74
Italy, 49–50, 95, 147

JAPAN, 50–54, 118, 131
Jasper, 128
Java, 47
Johnson, Samuel, 68
Jugs, 40–41, 91–92

Kagamibuta, 51
Kaji Tsunekichi, 54
Kamakura Daibutsu, 51
Kanabuta, 51
Kana-dari, 52
Kanazu Sorosaburo, 53
Kanomono, 52
K'ang Hsi, 33
K'ao kung chi, 32–33
Kashira, 51, fig. 2
Keir, James, 25
Keir's metal, 23, 25
Keisai, 53
Keswick, 41
Kettles, 17, 52, 53, 104–6
Keys, *see* Locks
Kinozoku-shi, 53
Kiribame, 52
Knockers, *see* Door knockers
Ku, 34
Kublai Khan, 31
Kuei, 34, fig. 1
Kumasi, 92
Kou Shou-Ching, 132

LA ROCHE, Sophie von, 108–9
La Tène, 29
Lacquer, 47, 64, 109

Lamps, 106–11
Langlois, Peter, 103
Lantern clocks, 134
Lanterns, 53, 111–12
Lapis Calaminaris, *see* Calamine
Lapis Lazuli, 128
Latten, 22, 79, 95, 138, 139
Le Mans, 72
Lecterns, 31, 45, 112–13
Leland, John, 42
Léonard, 37
Lichenberg, Georg, 76–77
Liège, 16, 31
Lighting appliances, 113–16
Limoges, 37, 97
Limousin, Leonard, 97
Lochana Buddha, 53
Lock plates, 116
Locks and keys, 116–18
Lough Gur, 39
Louis XIV, 76, 81, 102, 135
Louis XV, 38, 62, 76, 78, 81, 127, 147
Louis XVI, 38, 62, 78, 128, 147
Luristan bronzes, 48
'Lustre', 78, 82
Lü Ta-Lin, 33
Luttrell Psalter, 113

MALACHITE, 128
Mannheim gold, 26
Marquetry, 102
Meisonnier, Juste Aurele, 124
Menuki, 51, fig. 2
Metals, to clean, 149
Metropolitan Museum, New York, 49, 65, 74
Mica, 111
Michaelstow, 39
Microscopes, 118–19, 133
Milan Cathedral, 73
Milk Pails, 84
Mineral and Battery Works, 17, 41

INDEX

The Miner's Friend, 15
Mining for copper ores, 13–15, 31–32, 41, 42–43, 55
Mirrors, 26, 118–19
Monumental brasses, 119–31
More, Rev. Giles, 141
Mortars, 45, 92, 121
Mosaic gold, 26
Mosan brass, 30–31
Muntz, G. F., 23, 44
Muntz's metal, 23, 44
Murakani Takejoro, 53
Muscovy Glass, 111
Musical instruments, 121–3
Myddleton, Sir Richard, 117

NAGASAKA JURIJO, 53
National Button Society, 72
Nepal, 47
Netsuke, 51
Newcomen, Thomas, 15
Newton, Sir Isaac, 133
Nickel, 22, 25, 32
Nickel silver, 22, 44
Norwich, 113
Norwich Castle Museum, 105
Nottinghamshire, 16
Nuremburg, 38

OILS FOR BURNING, 115–16
Ojime, 51
Ophicleide, 122
Ormolu, 24, 37, 38, 42, 62, 68, 76, 77, 81, 94, 111, 134, 147, 149
  mounts on china, 123–6, 147–8
  mounts on furniture, 126–8
  mounts on marble and stone, 128–9

PADUA, 50
Paktong, 25, 32, 93
'Palais Royal', 125–6
Panchalouha, 27
Paraffin lamps, 111

Parvati, 46
Parys mountain, 42
Paschal Candlestick, 31, 73
Patina, 35–36
Péricaud, Nardon, 37
Phidias, 28
Phillipe le Bon, Duke of Burgundy, 31
Phoenicians, 28
Pinchbeck, 24–25
Pinchbeck, Christopher, 24
Pinchbeck, Edward, 24–25
Pins, 129–31
Pipes, Pipe-stoppers, 131
Pitchers, *see* Ewers and Jugs
Pocket-dials, 135
Pokers, 94
Polycandelon, 79
Porphyry, 128
Posnet, 136
Powder flasks, 131–2, fig. 8
Prabha, 46
Priapus, 106
Pricket, 75, 79
Prince's metal, 25–26
Pugin, Augustus Welby, 44
'Pull-up', 142
Pulpits, 55
Pumps for mining, 14–15
Purefoy, Henry, 115

'QUINQUETS', 108

RAG AND CHAIN PUMP, 14
Raymond, Pierre, 37
Regency furniture, 103
Revere, Paul, 62
Riccio, 50
Richard II, 41
Ring-dial, 135
Rococo, 38, 76, 78, 81, 123, 127
Roentgen, Abraham, 103
Rothschild Collection, 38
Royal Mint, 42

INDEX

Rupert of Bavaria, 25
Rush lights, 115
Russia, 42, 54–55

SALTRAM, 24
Samovars, 55
Sanseisha, 53
Saucepans, 136–7
Saunterings in and about London, 86–87
Savery, Thomas, 15
Scandinavia, 30, 40
Schlesinger, Max, 86–87
Scientific instruments, 132–6
'Sconce', 78
Seimin, 53
Serpent, 122
Sèvres, 123
Sextants, 133
Shaduko, 26
Shang-Yin, 35
Sheathing, 43–44
Sheffield plating, 44, 76
Shibuichi, 26
Ship-building, copper used in, 43–44
Ship Worm, 43
Shoe horns, 138
Shotwell and James, 72
Shovels, 94
Silver, 19, 22, 26, 27, 34, 44, 47, 49, 52, 65, 78, 81, 97, 105, 122, 131
Similor, 26
Skillets, 136–7
Skimmers, 137
Sligo, County, 39
Slodtz, 127
Smelting, 13, 15–16, 41
Snuffers, 88–89
Soho works, 42, 43, 68
Sokenshi, 51
Somerset, 16
Sōmin, 53

Spain, 42, 55, 66
Speculum, 26, 119
Spelter, 146
Spirit measures, 59–60
Spoons, 138–9
Stamping, 18–19, 43
'Steel', 26, 119
Stourbridge, 25
Student's lamp, 78
Sulphur, 16
Sulphuric acid, 13
Sumi-zōgan, 52
Sundials, 135
Surrey enamel, 19, 61
Swansea, 15
Sweden, 41, 55
Sword-mounting, 51
Syria, 48, 65

TAKUSAI, 53
Tallow candles, 114
Tea-kettles, 106
Teapots, 47, 105
Teestoofs, 67
Teijo, 53
Telescopes, 133
Thames, 66
Tibet, 47
Tin, 16, 21, 22, 23, 27, 28, 32, 47, 64
Ting, 34, fig 1
Tinning, 47–48, 137, 139
Tipton, 25
Tobacco boxes, 39, 139
Toledo, 55
Tombac, 26
Tongres, 31
Tongs, 94
Torbat, 67
Tortoiseshell, 103
Train oil, 116
Trivets, 94, 140–1, fig 9
Tsuba, 51, fig 2
Tuba, 122

INDEX

Tula, 54, 55
Tungshan Hills, 32
Turquoise, 47
Tutenag, 25, 32
Tylor and Sons, 84

VAN RIESENBURGH, 127
Venice, 55–56
Venus, 13
Victoria and Albert Museum, 24, 38, 39, 49, 54, 55, 56, 73, 74, 92, 120, 129, 140
Vischer, Hermann, 38
Vischer, Peter, 38
Vulliamy, Justin, 135

WADDESTON MANOR, 38
Wales, 15, 41, 42
Wallace Collection, 81, 129
Walpole, Horace, 97
Wang Fu, 33
Warming pans, 30, 141–2
Water-clocks, 133–4
Watt, James, 15, 42, 43, 68, 140
Wax-jacks, 142

Wedgewood, Josiah, 125
Weights and Measures, 142–3; *see also* Ale and Spirit Measures
Whitby Abbey, 65
White metal, 23
Whiteman, *see* Witeman
Wilkes, John, 117
Winchester, 97
Windsor Castle, 24, 25, 103, 129
Winfield, R W., 82–83
Wistar, Caspar, 71
Witeman, Henry, 71
Wool weights, 143–5

Yatate, 52
Yellow metal, 23
Yemen, 65
Yi-hsing stoneware, 105
Yoruba, 29
Yu, 34, fig. 1
Yunnan, 31, 32
Yuwakashi, 52

ZINC, 16, 17, 21, 22, 24, 25, 27, 30, 32, 33, 47, 146